BECOMING SELF-EMPLOYED

FIRST-HAND ADVICE
FROM THOSE WHO HAVE DONE IT!

SUSAN ELLIOTT

LIBERTY

FIRST EDITION

FIRST PRINTING

Copyright © 1987 by Live Oak Publications.

Printed in the United States of America

Reproduction or publication of the content in any manner, without express permission of the publisher, is prohibited. No liability is assumed with respect to the use of the information herein.

Published by:
  LIBERTY,
  A Division of
  TAB BOOKS Inc.
  P.O. Box 40
  Blue Ridge Summit, PA 17214

Library of Congress Cataloging in Publication Data

Elliott, Susan, 1950-
  Becoming self-employed.

  Bibliography: p.
  Includes index.
  1. Self-employed. I. Title.
HD8036.E44   1986   331.12′5   86-27205
ISBN 0-8306-3149-6 (pbk.)

Cover and text photos
courtesy of Tom Ellison

There is only one success . . .
to be able to spend your life
in your own way.

Christopher Morley

Contents

Not Just For Money:

Self-employment As a Way of Life

Visiting Denver's Larimar Square at Christmas time is a bit like stepping into one of those lovely Hallmark cards: streets blanketed in snow, cordoned off so shoppers can walk about freely; Chi-Chi restaurants and shops installed in restored turn-of-the-century storefronts in this historic section of town; lamp posts dressed with evergreen garlands and tiny lights. The merchants' association has hired Kay Casperson, among others, to provide the casual street entertainment of a winter carnival. On this afternoon two days before Christmas, it is very cold, the mercury hovering around freezing. The streets are packed with a thick mat of crunchy snow. Most of the crowds have gone home for dinner but Kay still has a while to go before her contracted time is up. A conscientious worker, she goes out to finish her last hour.

She pulls on an oversized trollish costume with funny feet and long arms that can grow and grow. The whole street is her stage. At first there is a little crowd and a group of musicians working with her, but eventually the cold drives the shoppers indoors and the musicians' fingers start to freeze. Kay, snug inside the furry costume, continues alone. As she dances, a phenomenon well known to performers occurs: she is completely absorbed in the character, losing track of both audience and time. Emerging momentarily from her concentration, she realizes that the time has flown and her day is over.

Kay looks up now to find that the street is empty save for a little boy and his little dog, both watching, mesmerized. She turns and looks down the street; dusk has begun to settle over the city and the lights are just coming up. She thinks, "What a strange way to end the day with this audience of two." Then, sensing something above her, she glances up to see perhaps 150 office workers leaning from their second-story windows. All at once their applause fills the street.

Somehow there's a lesson to be drawn from this little incident. Like Kay, anyone seeking self-employment must force himself out into a cold, unwelcoming environment. Like Kay, most entrepreneurs experience a period when it seems that the marketplace is all but ignoring their efforts. But, again like Kay, if you can concentrate on doing your very best work — and especially if you can become totally absorbed in what you're doing and persevere in spite of limited initial response from your customers — the odds of a happy outcome are surprisingly good.

You might question whether the analogy really holds up. First, is a freelance performer like Kay truly an entrepreneur? Second, considering small business failure rates, aren't the odds of survival pretty slim?

WHO IS AN ENTREPRENEUR?

It's true that Kay Casperson doesn't fit the media's image of an entrepreneur. She's not another Ted Turner, wheeling and dealing and creating business empires with only a handshake. But if you look at the critical issues of control, responsibility and self-determination it's clear that Kay and everyone else interviewed for this book is an entrepreneur in his or her own right.

The problem with the popular, media-inspired image of entrepreneurs is that it's easy to forget that the image is an illusion. We begin to believe that people who go into business for themselves are either fabulously successful . . . or end up bankrupt. The image persists in spite of the reality, which is that most people are neither complete successes nor complete failures in business. In reality, how we feel about what we get from a venture depends as much on what we're expecting as on the much overrated "bottom line."

The people interviewed in this book, like most people, are smart enough not to want to win at any price. Becoming a grim success in business is really no success at all, and they know it. These are people who are concerned foremost with creating an independent *livelihood*, which is much more than simply an independent income.

Motivations for choosing independence vary. For some it's self-expression; Kay Casperson would probably list this first. Some enjoy the almost magical process of nurturing a project all the way from idea to reality. As innkeeper Emily Hunter says, "I want to have visualized something and been right about it. That's the ongoing challenge for me."

Kay Casperson
Performer/Mime

Work satisfaction is often mentioned as a motivation for becoming self-employed. As baker Warren Paul says, "For me, money is not enough reason to work as hard as I do. I can do a lot of things to make money. I have to enjoy what I'm doing."

Others want to invest in themselves rather than invest their time and energies building a business for someone else. As a hardworking antique dealer put it, "It's like renting a house — finally you think, 'Why not buy?'"

Self-employment is seen by some as a way to involve the whole family in a shared venture — a way to build family bonds and instill values. Still others are primarily interested in quality personal contact; they seek businesses in which they can establish friendships and relate to people in meaningful ways.

THE TRUTH ABOUT BUSINESS FAILURE RATES

In an article entitled "Numbers That Lie," economist Albert Shapero notes that "One of the biggest barriers to entrepreneurship is the widespread notion that almost all new businesses fail in very short order. This myth discourages young people who might think of going into business for themselves, and it influences important people who affect start-ups, like bankers, government officials and professors (who ought to know better)."

One problem in estimating success rates is that the available figures are incomplete. Dun & Bradstreet, the source used by many government publications, keeps track of fewer than one-third of the 14 million U.S. companies. Another difficulty lies in deciding what constitutes a "failure." Bankruptcy, itself not necessarily a death knell, is only one reason a business might close. The owners might retire, or might simply lose interest and go on to something new. Can these be considered failures? Besides, who knows how many successful entrepreneurs failed on the first try only to learn from their mistakes, gather their resources and make it on the second or third try? Clearly statistics on small business failure rates don't always paint an accurate picture.

ABOUT THE PEOPLE IN THIS BOOK

With the current glut of how-to books and success seminars, there is no shortage of enticement for starting your own business. Perhaps the thing that distinguishes this book is that it has no particular axe to grind. The entrepreneurs simply tell their stories, candidly sharing the good with the bad, the rewards along with the disappointments. They share their biggest triumphs as well as their most regretted mistakes. Through them you'll get an inside view into the lives of the self-employed and come away with a much clearer picture of where you yourself stand.

None of the people in this book are extremely rich or famous. They're *real* people, and because of that they are good role models. We can look at the livelihoods they've created for themselves and know that, given enough imagination and determination, we too can be fully, joyfully independent.

The Attainable Dream

"It sounds like bragging, but I know from experience that there's no other restaurant where you get as many people walking out saying 'This is the best meal I've ever had in my life.' That, to me, is worth it right there." Customer accolades might well be enough for Brian Finn, a 25-year-old former marine biology student, but the truth is, running the Gold Hill Inn pays a generous cluster of dividends.

With a population that just nudges 150, Gold Hill is nestled in a mountain meadow surrounded by the ranges of the Continental Divide. The road into town is both formidable and breathtaking. Barely wide enough for two jeeps to pass, it winds back and forth against the mountain, offering a spectacular view of Long's Peak and Horsfal Mountain — and a harrowing drop into the canyon below. But on weekend nights, cars line both sides of the town's main road. The restaurant, explains Brian's brother Chris, is Gold Hill's only real attraction. The only other businesses are a little general store and the antique shop across from the inn. "We don't want to promote the town," he says. "We want it to stay just the way it is.

"It's a unique place," explains Brian. "It draws people who want to get away from the crowd where they won't be recognized." People like Gary Hart,

Judd Hirsch and William Shatner. Film critic Roger Ebert has dined there three times.

Brian Finn
Gold Hill Inn

They certainly don't come for the sumptuous accoutrements. The lodge looks much the same as it did when the Finns found it: open rafters, bare wood floors, three giant rock fireplaces. None of the tables or chairs match, nor do the plates or silverware. Linens? "Whenever there's a sale on printed sheets," says Chris, "we buy those and cut 'em up for tablecloths and napkins." The dress code runs to the casual side. "Some people come in their tuxes, but if you want to come in with your hiking boots and shorts that's fine."

If customers don't come for an elegant dining experience, what do they hazard ten miles of twisting mountain road for? "One of the best meals you've ever eaten," replies Brian, grinning broadly. The Gold Hill Inn is a four-star restaurant, written up in *Fortune Magazine* and rated in the top one hundred Colorado restaurants by *Colorado Gourmet Gold*.

The fare — not in the least what you'd expect to find in a mining camp — is an ecclectic spread Chris calls "mixed homemade," a testament to the family's Irish hospitality. The roughly 150 nightly dinners are served *table d' hote*, a seven-course, two-hour feast. Diners can choose from appetizers such as smoked trout or steak tartare, or a tofu bean plate. The *soup du jour* might be cock-a-leekie or cream of peanut, served with fresh-baked breads that range from Boston Brown to Pan Blanco to egg bagels. Entrées include old favorites like steak and kidney pie and Lobster Newburg and for the adventurous, Buffalo Wellington and exotic Pheasant Sweetbreads. Desserts stir the imagination: There is a custard called "Floating Ireland," and "Red Hoss Mountain," a frozen strawberry mousse.

Chris Finn is the chef. "I learned to cook right here in the restaurant. I started when I was about nine, helping Mom with the baking and whatever needed to be done." The picture is priceless. Chris is a very tall, very thin 29-year-old, with shoulder-length hair, ratty jeans, T-shirt and rubber boots. *This* is the chef of this acclaimed restaurant? Like everything else, it fits.

Brian and Chris will unhesitatingly say that their goal in running the Gold Hill Inn is to please the people who come for dinner, not to get rich in the restaurant busines. "We're here to make a living," says Chris. "That's all. Just make a living, not make a fortune. We'd rather give people a good meal for a reasonable price and have them be happy. As long as we can get by, that's all that matters."

"The quality is important," he continues. "It's serving the people something they can't get anyplace else. I've cooked at other restaurants and the thing I hate is you've got this set menu; you've got to do the same thing every day, just do it faster. Up here I have freedom." There is no printed menu. Instead, a chalkboard out front lists the evening's bill of fare. That way, if Chris finds something good in a magazine and wants to try it that weekend, he can. "I can do whatever I want as long as it's good."

"And the quality goes beyond the food," adds Brian. "You have the atmosphere. Working for yourself you have the freedom to be as hospitable as you'd like. For example, we never hesitate to give free drinks. People aren't used to that because so many restaurants are run on a strictly business level."

"We do minimal advertising," Brian continues. "We depend on our reputation. We have two different couples who were our first customers ever and they still come back." Seeing people come back year after year, they must have grown quite friendly with some, must have had some memorable experiences. Chris nods. "Well, that happens a lot. The best anniversary dessert I ever did was for the Ellsworth's 50th anniversary. I wanted to do Peaches Flambé, and there were no raspberries. Luckily it was August and I knew where to go up here along the road to find wild raspberries. At the end of the night they were talking with Mom and Dad and Mrs. Ellsworth asked Mom, 'Where did you get those wild raspberries?' She knew."

The Finns feel a great sense of pride in running their unique, highly respected restaurant. In fact, they say that when asked what they do, the simple response, "We run the Gold Hill Inn" is enough said. "Maybe what keeps us going is the ego booster of the whole place," remarks Brian. "It *is* an ego boost, and everybody needs one."

What do they see themselves doing in five years? "I'll be pleased to be right here," replies Chris, to which Brian nods agreement. After all, they point out, "It's basically the ideal lifestyle."

WORK YOU CAN LOVE

It should come as no surprise that most people are dissatisfied with their jobs. Department of Health, Education and Welfare studies reveal that over half of all white collar workers and almost two-thirds of all blue collar workers would choose different occupations if they had it to do over again. Conduct your own informal survey and you'll probably find that almost everyone you know has a dream job, something else he'd rather do, if not now, then "someday" when circumstances are different. Usually, that dream job is marked by three characteristics:

- It is meaningful work.

- It is fulfilling. It contributes to family and personal goals rather than conflicting with them.

- It provides a sense of being in control, of offering independence and freedom of both lifestyle and destiny.

Generally speaking, this combination is found only in self-employment, which accounts for the huge numbers of people who want to switch from employee to entrepreneur — not only want to switch, *are* switching. Again, conduct your own research: A look around your own town will bear out government statistics that show self-employment is growing at an ever-increasing pace.

Of course some employees are locked into their jobs for various reasons such as debt or poor health. For others, the biggest obstacle to independence may simply be inertia. The biggest difference between the doers and the dreamers, however, seems to be perception — perception of the dream and perception of self.

• Most people who consider self-employment to be an unattainable fantasy have misconceptions about what it takes to succeed. They tend to overrate startup capital and to underrate such factors as planning, perseverance and determination. The entrepreneurial stereotype is frequently an obstacle.

• Many people misjudge their own capabilities. They tend to measure themselves by inappropriate standard or to exaggerate the differences (in education, experience, native intelligence) between themselves and their employers.

• While most people like the idea of an independent lifestyle, other things — such as security — are sometimes valued more highly.

MEASURING YOURSELF AGAINST THE RIGHT YARDSTICK

"Anybody who's in business is in business because he doesn't like the game — the game being getting in good with the boss, trying to make a buck."
                                                                Bill Felder

If you are a serious candidate for self-employment, chances are you've felt uncomfortable working for others. Entrepreneurs are frequently people who don't seem able to succeed in the corporate environment, not because they lack ability, but because they don't fit easily into the system. Sadly, some of these people mistakenly conclude that there is something wrong with them. Assuming that you're not cut out for business because you are a dismal failure as an accountant or as a junior salesman isn't fair to yourself; nor is it realistic. It could well be that you're simply in the wrong position, that the same qualities that cause sparks to fly in the office may be the very ones that would make you highly successful out on your own.
   How do you know if you're a good candidate for self-employment? You might start by comparing yourself with the entrepreneurs in this book. As heterogeneous a group as they are where age, sex, education and background are concerned, they all have certain traits in common.

- Independence, Non-conformity

The need for autonomy is a strong part of the entrepreneurial makeup. Very few entrepreneurs can easily tolerate being told what to do or even tolerate being closely supervised. For these people, freedom to "do it my own way" is a basic requirement for job satisfaction.

- Strong Leadership Qualities

"An entrepreneur is usually not a team player — unless he can be the captain," writes David Hasley in *Starting Up*. Most would rather be solely responsible for the success or failure of a project than share responsibility with a committee.

- Self-confidence, Initiative

Entrepreneurs aren't afraid to act on their decisions. Bill Felder says, "I'm opinionated. I have answers for people before they have questions." This trait, or the viewpoint that your own ideas and abilities are at least as worthy as the boss', can be a real source of friction. Corporate managers are often bewildered and threatened by behavior they label "impertinent" or "insubordinate," while these concepts have little relevance to the goal-oriented entrepreneur.

- Determination, Tenacity

While talent and creativity are great assets, it's often sheer perseverance that separates the successes from the failures.

- Flexibility

Entrepreneurs are often "divergent thinkers." Fast on their feet, they enjoy problem solving and typically see opportunities where others see obstacles.

- Multiple Talents

Small business owners typically wear a lot of different hats, and many entrepreneurs thrive on the variety in their daily lives. As potter John Hansen puts it, "There are so many things involved in running a business that require different personality traits and different skills. If you've done one thing for ten years, as a cog in the wheel, you probably haven't had the chance to develop those skills. I think that one of the advantages of a self-sufficient lifetyle is that you acquire a whole circle of skills and abilities and the chance to exercise them."

As we'll see, many of the people in this book broke out of jobs they found too confining in order to structure new careers with room for growth in new — possibly several new — directions. They have either chosen businesses that require multiple skills or they've created multi-faceted businesses. This is certainly true for Tom Haworth and his family, and for Charlotte Elich-McCall.

TOM AND JUDY HAWORTH,
THE VINTAGE TOWERS INN

"I have to be on my own," says Tom Haworth, who with his wife, Judy, owns a charming country inn, a Victorian cameo set in the foothills of Sonoma County, California. For Tom, being on his own means "no one telling me what to do. I'm just full of ideas and I want to pursue them and see the fruits of my labors. We're entrepreneurs — dyed in the wool."

The building process itself has been a particular satisfaction for the Haworths. "Everybody wants to feel they're the only ones who could have pulled it off, but you have to remember that we came to a town that had nothing really going for it." At the turn of the century, Tom explains, the village of Cloverdale was a tourist mecca with more than a hundred fine hotels. But as California developed its excellent highway system and cars became commonplace, travelers drifted to other vacation spots. Mendicino, for example, is only an hour and a half away. So when Tom and Judy bought the doctor's residence that was to become the Vintage Towers Inn, "it was a town that hadn't yet started to happen. We were the first tourist-oriented business to come along in years."

What Tom and Judy saw were abundant possibilities: a one-of-a-kind dwelling surrounded by oak and pine forests, "plus there's a river that flows right by; you can take canoes all the way to the ocean. The only thing the town lacked was quality lodging. So we took the gamble and put our money into this wonderful building."

Making the necessary renovations on a shoestring budget was the hardest part, Tom says. "We didn't have a half million dollars to spend on the inn so we had to do most of it ourselves. We had to do it very circumspectly; we opened four rooms first, then restored three more and added more baths.

"It was a lot of work. With five bathrooms to install and the only plumber in town retiring, I had to learn to be a plumber. Every room has been redecorated; we laid new carpet, used the best paints and wallpapers. My wife and I did everything but the air conditioning and the roof."

Tom cautions that inkeeping is one business that requres capital. "I think someone with $200,000 could make a successful inn work, but the idea that you can get in for $50,000 is probably not realistic. I guess it depends on where you are. I guess you could buy an old house in Arkansas for $50,000 but in California you don't buy an old house for that kind of money — $300,000 maybe, with $100,000 down. That would leave you $100,000 to put into the restoration."

At any rate, the Haworth's $200,000 gamble has paid off. "We've got five years work in the place and it's grossing a real substantial income for us now. It's going to pay for our daughters' college if it keeps going like it is." Finally, Tom notes with understandable pride, the Vintage Tower Inn has been added to the national registry of historic buildings. "That's something we're proud of, getting that through all by ourselves."

THRIVING ON RESPONSIBILITY: CHARLOTTE ELICH-McCALL

Charlotte Elich-McCall launched Skyloom Fibers after working five years as the office manager in an automotive repair service. Quite a leap, she admits, even given her clearly impulsive style, but one she's never regretted. "The last year I worked at the automotive service, I heard about a weaving class, and since I'd knitted since I was six years old, I thought I'd like to try it." Charlotte found that she really enjoyed the craft, so much so that when she later heard about a local weaving shop going up for sale, she decided to look into it.

"What I discovered was that there were all kinds of things I wanted to change. It didn't seem like they had a very good location and they had a funny balance of inventory. They had more money in beads and things like belt buckles and not very much in yarn. I decided that if I wanted to change that much about it, maybe I should just start my own store.

"My boss, whom I had a very good relationship with, was looking for tax write-offs then — especially for a real estate write-off. When he and I found this building, he bought it and leased it to me."

Talking with Charlotte today, it doesn't seem at all surprising that her former boss should place so much confidence in her. At thirty, she appears extremely self-assured, quite capable of running one of the largest weaving stores in the country. It *is* a little amazing, though, when you consider that Charlotte was only 23 when she set up shop. She must have shown unusual maturity and initiative even then. "When I started working for Ray I was nineteen. I got the job because my father knew him. My father is a barber and used to cut his hair. I guess Ray was sitting in my dad's shop one day and just mentioned that he needed some help. At the time I had just quit college and I was working in a fabric store. My dad made the comment, 'I know just the person for you and she likes to work' — I guess that was my dad's image of me — anyway, he and I went down one Sunday morning and talked to Ray and I started only two weeks later.

"I really attribute a lot to the way he gave me responsibility. I mean, at nineteen, I knew when I was working at the fabric store that maybe I had a lot more on the ball than a lot of the people working there, but it was real frustrating because you could do what they wanted and do a good job of it but you never got any rewards. All you got was your nickel an hour raise every six months. That sort of gets depressing. When I first started working with Ray, I was there only about a week and he gave me a quarter raise — that was something new to me.

Charlotte Elich-McCall, Skyloom Fibers

"He gave me a lot of responsibility. He told me he felt he could leave the place with me in charge and feel confident about it. Because I had all that responsibility, I felt more confidence in myself. Another thing was that in that business I had to prove myself all the time. Being a woman, selling automotive parts, all I dealt with were men who immediately assumed that I didn't know anything. So I got a lot of business training from Ray — a seat-of-your-pants kind of business training."

Consequently, even at 23 Charlotte had a reasonably solid foundation. She knew enough, for example, to do some research before jumping into her own business. "I had different trade magazines and weaving magazines and I just started writing letters, gathering all kinds of informaton, addresses and so forth. Also, there was another weaving shop in town. I had been in there and had an idea of the kind of stock they carried." A couple of months later a location for the shop was found, but the building did require remodeling. "It was an upholstery shop before for thirty-some years so it was pretty ratty."

Fortunately, Charlotte had some willing helpers; her mother, sister, and two male friends made up the "destruction and remodeling crew." They all worked on the building at night and in their spare time. "My goal was to open October 22, and I made that goal. I had a lot of help from this one boyfriend. He would sit down with me at night and go over different kinds of materials and see what I wanted. Not knowing what you need or anything, you make a few mistakes, but I have to say, I think my instincts were pretty good; I still carry a lot of inventory that I chose when I first started.

Charlotte is now exploring new directions for Skyloom Fibers, which is already one of the largest stores of its kind in the country. A move to a new location is scheduled and a mail-order catalog is currently in the idea and planning stage.

Declarations of Independence

Control. It can mean any number of things, ranging from choice in the day-to-day details of your life to freedom of career direction and ultimate control over your personal destiny. Without exception those interviewed for this book consider basic autonomy to be absolutely essential in their own pursuit of happiness.

CONTROLLING YOUR WORK/CONTROLLING YOUR LIFE

"The company was going through some changes — changes that were affecting my career and my life — and I didn't like it," states gallery owner Joan Robey, a forceful, energetic woman who doesn't take much of anything lying down. "I said 'Wait a minute! If this guy in Tulsa can make a decision that has this kind of effect on my life, then why can't I? I mean if this guy can decide what to do with thousands of people in this huge company, why can't I make decisions about a couple of people in a small business of my own? What's *he* got that I don't?'"

Who hasn't looked at his boss and thought, "If I were in his/her shoes, I could do at least as well — maybe better?" But somehow that thought is seldom translated into action. "As often as I had thought about someday starting my own business, it always seemed like such an enormous thing to do that it had no relation to reality," says Joan. It was only after her sense of self-directedness was affronted that she began to look seriously at the idea. At that point, she examined some of the assumptions she'd accepted, notably the presumed differences between herself and "this guy in Tulsa," and found that the differences weren't as great as she'd supposed. "Sure, he was a little older and more experienced and blah, blah, blah — but I also have some good experience and a really good sense about people and business. Suddenly this gap between someone else's owning a business and my owning my own business diminished (clapping her hands) like that. I thought, 'If he can do it, I can do it.'"

"Why Let Someone Else Have the Glory?"

"It seemed I was finally in the right place at the right time so I asked myself, 'Well, what's it going to be? If your dream is to have your own business, what would it take to make the dream come true?' When I decided to just forget about all the 'shoulds' and really explore my fantasy, the concept of this gallery started to take shape."

At first Joan was nearly overcome with conflicting hopes and anxieties. One moment she felt ready to take the business world by storm; the next, fairly paralyzed with self-doubt. "I couldn't eat, sleep — couldn't think of anything else. I took people to lunch or for a drink — anyone and everyone I knew in the retail business, anyone who had started his own business, anyone associated with the arts — and especially anyone I knew who might convince me not to go ahead. I asked a lot of questions: Where do I start? Where do I go to get financing? Do I go buy art or find a location first? I mean, what if it took me six months to find a location — would I have a house full of boxes in the meantime? Really, I didn't know the first thing about opening a gallery."

Things were further complicated when a friend offered Joan a partnership in his restaurant. She admits the idea was tempting; it would certainly be less risky going into an established busienss with someone who'd already been at it ten years. Joan remembers thinking, "That sounds good; I can sort of do it, but sort of not do it.

"Finally I said 'I'm going away!' I went to Mexico and lay on the beach and read novels; completely disassociated myself from the whole thing. After five days I got on the plane knowing exactly what I was going to do. I came home and announced to everybody, including myself, 'I AM OPENING THIS GALLERY!' Why come all this way in life, have this dream of opening your own business and then cop out at the final goal line? Why give someone else the glory?"

Warren Paul, Cheesecakes and More

Taking charge required a little less turmoil for Warren Paul, a former legislative assistant who found himself unemployed in the wake of budget cuts. "It had nothing to do with whether you were good or not," Warren recalls. "They said, 'You're doing real good stuff but for all these reasons, the funding for your job's been cut.'" Warren made up his mind to find a livelihood in which success or failure would depend strictly on his own merits rather than on bureaucratic caprice. "I had to have control over that. I have to be able to decide on my own whether I'm going to make it or not." The results? His own booming retail and wholesale bakery.

Paul, a dynamic, voluble Italian who loves people as much as he does baking, was fairly submerged in rounds of job interviews when he remembered a friend in New York who happened to have a "to-die-for" recipe for authentic Italian cheesecake. When the friend agreed to let Warren use the recipe, Warren immediately envisioned himself the producer of no less than the best cheesecake in town, a goal, his fans would argue, he's long since achieved. Starting in his home with a $200 investment in baking pans, it wasn't long before his accounts included many of the poshest restaurants in town. Warren proudly tells of one couple who regularly makes a 20-mile pilgrimage for a half-pound of his "Diplomat Cake."

Warren Paul, Cheesecakes & More

"Quality is my main thing," explains Paul. "I'm not big enough that I can sell 20,000 cakes in a day." In fact, he says, he wouldn"t want to pursue a huge restaurant or supermarket account that might come to comprise a third of his business. For one thing, it would be risky: what if he should lose an account that size? Besides, such a big customer would have too much leverage. It would not be unlike working for someone else.

THE FRUITS OF THEIR OWN LABORS

Pauli Wanderer had worked for other antique dealers several years before "sick of working for other people," she took the plunge into her own business. "I was a really good salesperson," she says. "People could leave their store with me for a week and be confident that things would be run properly. But here I was, putting in the hours, investing in the place as if it were my own, yet drawing a salary that was barely over minimum wage. It's like renting a house — finally you think, 'Why not buy?' Why not have my efforts go into something of my own?'"

Doing it Your Own Way

Entrepreneurs typically believe that self-employment is the only way to go for the self-starting idea person. Working for yourself offers two great advantages:

• You can use your own ideas, do things your way and see the stamp of your individuality on the outcome.

• Your are free to change direction at any time; you can devise a business that utilizes many of your talents or can pursue several different interests at once.

Donna Hudgel recalls that before opening her own bookstore, she's never had any book selling experience. "I didn't really know anything about how a bookstore works," she says. "I thought it might be a good idea, before I took the plunge, to work for another bookstore and find out more about it. So I spent a day walking around town visting all the bookstores, trying to find one I thought I'd be comfortable working in." To her dismay, Donna couldn't find a single one that seemed to fill the bill. "I could see something I didn't like in every one of the stores; I knew I wouldn't be able to do it the way they were doing it. I thought to myself, 'Oh dear, what do I do now?' The answer was, 'Well, I'll just open my own store and do it my way.'"

"Doing it my way" is a must for freelance chef Bill Felder, who says, "The biggest payoff for me is just being able to work for myself. I'm not a corporate person — I have too many ideas about how things should be. When I work for myself I set my own standards.

"I'm my own worst critic," says Felder. "If you can't put out a meal that you think is great, if it's not the way you visualize it, then it doesn't matter what the folks at the table think. Oh I'm glad they enjoyed it; that's nice. But the truth is I don't cook for other people — I cook for me.

"I like catering," Felder continues, adding his opinion that it's the only operation in the food business that makes sense." The reason, he explains, is catering is the only operation in which he feels he's in control. "In a restaurant, the customer's always in control. First you have to worry, is he going to come in? And when he comes in, is he going to order the roast beef or the steak and kidney pie? Do I make an extra roast beef or an extra pie? If it snows that night, what do I do with the leftover?

"In a catering situation you know that Tuesday at 12:30 you're having a luncheon for 35 of Mrs. Smith's nearest and dearest and you're going to have tenderloin sandwiches. And you also know that on Thursday you're going to have a cocktail party for Mr. Jones at 7 in the evening and that the leftover tenderloin can be reground and made into stuffing for the mushroom caps. And if something goes wrong you can offer him a second drink and say it'll be another ten minutes. You have the control."

Seeing Your Stamp on the End Product

Potter John Hansen agrees that maintaining control of your work is essential. "Being in control of the various aspects of a job gives you an outlet you wouldn't have if you were just one cog of a large wheel," he says. Hansen's commercial specialty is a large, hand-carved, hand-painted stein sold in mountain resort gift shops. "There's a certain sense of pride in doing all this and making it work. This is me. It's not like tightening this nut on this car frame — you have no personal investment in something like that.

"I'm spoiled," he grins. "To go back to something where you can't really see your imprint on the final product would be very tough after doing this."

CONTROLLING CAREER DIRECTION

Working for yourself, you're not pidgeonholed, not locked into anything. This is particularly important for entrepreneurs such as writer/lecturer Betsy Morscher, whose business has taken different forms at different times. "I found a corporate structure very constraining," she says. "I have never allowed anything to become a fulltime business because I have such diversified interests. I remember neighbors saying to me 'Betsy, you're so flighty. You must be brain damaged because you can't stay with any one thing.' My answer to that was, 'But if you look at my track record you'll see that everything I've done has been done very well.'"

Freedom to change is likewise one of Joan Robey's delights. "It's hard for me to sit still. I have a lot of energy and a lot of ideas. I'm already working on some ideas for expansion. This is definitely a long-term commitment, but I'm at total liberty to change it: grow it, shrink it, have it look a different way, open up another one and have it be a little different, whatever."

No More Committees

Meg Biddle, From "Interim President" to Cartoonist

"I was sick and tired of sitting on my butt, having meeting after meeting that didn't seem to go anywhere," says artist Meg Biddle. "I was representing everybody else when I really wanted to do something for myself." It took courage and planning but Meg at last broke out of the committee room in order to pursue a long-delayed dream of a career in art. The inspiring thing about her move was that in returning to the work she loved, Meg proved that no dream, regardless of how bizarre or improbable it may seem to others, is necessarily beyond reach.

"I'm an Army brat," begins Meg. "I went to school outside Philadelphia and when I was about nineteen I left for California to study at the California College of Arts and Crafts. At college I studied all fine art — no commercial art at all — and I was very strict about that with myself and everybody else. ('Well, *this* is art . . . and commercial art — that's something else.') The result was I graduated with a bachelor of fine arts and was totally unemployable."

For a number of years Meg worked outside the field of art, trying all kinds of businesses. "I was in commercial real estate for a while. Finally, I ended up in this company called Performance Technology, a clearinghouse for inventors of building processes and new kinds of solar energy. We were pulling together investors and just about the time it started rolling, about the time we should have stepped down and let managers handle it, I found myself stuck in the job of interim president. I kept wanting to step down and they wouldn't let me; it kept going on and on and I got real strung out. Finally I said, 'Give me a leave of absence and don't call me.' They agreed to that.

"I was no sooner out the door on my ostensible month's leave than I went straight to this place called Better Jobs for Women, an employment agency that helped women get into non-traditional fields. This is how hungry I was for something different. When the counselor asked what I'd like to do, I said, 'Well, this is going to throw you but I'd like to be doing cartoon books.'"

To Meg's surprise, the counselor merely asked, "Why aren't you doing it?" That question became the turning point.

Although it took some prodding at first, Meg quickly came up with a portfolio which she showed to people in the cartooning business, purposely avoiding friends who might give slanted opinions. "The response was wonderful. I felt like a million bucks."

Suddenly Meg was back in the art world, albeit in a very different facet from what she'd envisioned in her student days. What counted was that she was doing what she wanted to do. However, there was still her old company to reckon with. "We had a board meeting and I went in feeling great. They noticed the improvement in me and naturally thought, 'That time off has been great for her; now she can get back to work.' Instead I handed out my resignation and said I wouldn't be able to continue as interim president — or anything else. 'You see, I'm going to be much too busy cartooning.'"

The board members' reaction was just what Meg had anticipated:

"Cartooning?!"

"What's going on?"

"She's taken drugs!"

After five years, Meg is more convinced than ever that she made the right decision and has loved watching her reputation grow every year. "I decided this time I'm not going to blow it. Not a chance; this feels too good. I can go and have my adventures now and it's not only not detrimental to my work, it's actually an asset. In fact," she says gleefully, "I can write it off.

"I truly want to be responsible for just myself," Meg says. "I'm confident about charting my own course when I'm the only one affected. If I take a risk, it's going to be only me taking that risk. I'm not going to have to have a meeting and vote on it."

Ralph Jackson, Consulting Engineer

"He travels fastest who travels alone" might well be the motto of corporate dropouts who relish their newfound autonomy, particularly where decision making is concerned. On his own now, Ralph Jackson looks back at his public transportation agency days and wonders that he accomplished as much as he did. "Probably the biggest source of frustration in an organization with a 15-member board of directors and a general manager and several department heads is that you spend most of your time just trying to put things together. You were constantly challenged to get other people to understand what needed to be done and to somehow motivate them to do that. I'm one of those people — I guess because I'm an engineer — that when I reason something through and it makes sense to me, that's what (I'm convinced) we ought to do. The frustration of taking that through the bureaucracy was maddening; many times you'd lose the opportunity that was originally there just because it took too long to come to a decision."

Ralph Jackson is so down-to-earth he makes it easy to forget his titles; when you gradually become aware of how remarkable he is, it's because of the open, matter-of-fact way he talks about his accomplishments. He harbors no false modesty; obviously he's well aware of his abilities and takes quiet pride in the way his business and family life have turned out. At the same time, there's no grandstanding, no condescension toward others. Jackson clearly feels happy about the decisions he's made and his easy, relaxed posture quickly puts others at ease. He enjoys talking about his business.

"Strategic planning and computer programming is probably the simplest way to put it," he says. "What that means is, the last couple of years that I was with the agency I worked with the board of directors to decide whether or not they were accomplishing the things they intended to do. One element of my business now is helping smaller companies who don't have my kind of expertise do that same kind of strategic planning. It may be a company that's doing reasonably well right now but they don't know whether they want to expand or not, or what would happen if they did.

"A second, almost completely independent area is related to developing software for the travel industry. I just returned from five weeks in Israel, where I completely computerized a tour operation over there. It was a fairly complex operation that they just couldn't keep track of on a manual system. I'm developing the software to the point where I can market it to travel agencies here.

"The third major chunk right now is my work with two large transportation engineering consulting firms. I either become a part of their team, or on a couple of projects, I become the project manager for them on a contract basis. It's kind of a mixed bag."

A question that naturally arises is why Jackson left his top level position with the agency. As deputy executive director, he was number two in authority to the general manager, with responsibility for managing an annual construction budget of around a hundred million dollars. What prompted him to leave such a job?

"I'd been with the agency for 14 years and it was time to leave. I felt that and they felt that. There were two things, really: one was very pragmatic, that I had advanced in their salary structure to the point where I was making almost as much as the general manager — just under $60,000 a year." Jackson explains that money wasn't the issue, *per se*, but the fact that nothing he did could affect his earnings made him lose incentive. "I'd been in my current job for three or four years. I'd go to the general manager and say, 'I want a bigger challenge; I want an opportunity to grow.' and he'd say 'You're making what I'm making — there's no place for you to go.'

"I needed to leave there, the question was what to do and where to go. I didn't really want to get back into another large transit operation, involved at the top with the public and everything else. So the decision was to start my own company."

At the top, he must have enjoyed quite a bit of freedom and control, not to mention prestige. Was it really so bad working for a big agency? "There were pluses and minuses," replies Jackson. "On the plus side, it was a large company with a lot of resources. If you decided to buy a computer and somebody else agreed, then you'd go and buy a computer. If you wanted some more software, you'd go get some software." The negative side was the frustration of trying to get things done in a system of department heads that could be extremely resistant to change.

"Another thing I learned after 14 years was that even though I spent a lot of time in management, I didn't particularly enjoy managing other people. I'm not particularly good at confronting people, especially when there's a performance or behavioral problem. I frequently will just avoid those kinds of situations. I find it much more enjoyable plugging away doing my own thing and not having to worry about a bunch of other people."

Jackson mentions that probably the major change since being on his own is the way he's come to perceive time. He's very aware now of "billable hours." Because of that, he's come to value both his time and his skills much more than in the past. "The constant challenge is to increase your productivity, to get more done in the same amount of time. And I'm probably a better employee for whoever I'm working for because of that. I have also found that I can be very productive when I decide that's what I want to do.

"The other thing is, when you start going out and telling a client what your're charging him per hour you learn that you really are worth quite a bit to people and they're willing to pay that for your services."

He notes that $50 an hour may sound like a lot of money until you consider his overhead: business car, computer, all the expenses that occur in his operation; the profits are trimmed very quickly. He's had to find ways of keeping costs down. "I worked out a relationship with a friend who owns an office building. I work one day a week for him on some development projects of his in exchange for office, telephones, Xerox machines, secretarial support and those kinds of things."

The shift to his own business has brought Jackson new flexibility, greater control and greater opportunity for growth. Even more importantly, the business has become a facilitator rather than an obstacle to achieving the kind of family life he wants.

Patrish Wiggens, "The Velvet Touch"

Patrish is the quintessential white collar dropout. Her business, which she's named The Velvet Touch, speaks eloquently of what matters to her: the freedom of being "in the driver's seat," the challenge of selling herself and the joy of creative expression. In her late thirties, with dark-blond hair, crinkly smile lines around the eyes and the small trim figure of a much younger woman, Patrish exudes enthusiasm, as if every experience is a potential adventure, every acquaintance a budding friendship. She travels light; three years ago sold everything she owned in a garage sale. All the better, she maintains, to move — and move quickly — in whatever direction her venture takes her. What business could instill a person with such a zest for living? Patrish owns a shoe shine service.

Actually, The Velvet Touch is several services in one, Patrish explains. In addition to shoe shines, she also offers pedicure and reflexology, a wonderful therapeutic foot massage that leaves the feet warm and tingling, the mind and body relaxed and refreshed. A massage generally lasts an hour and a half; as she works, one immediately notices the uncommon strength in her hands. She operates out of her home, where an honest-to-goodness shoe shine stand perches high on a wooden platform in one corner of her living room.

Patrish's evolution from retail buyer for the May Company to independent shoe shine magnate began several years ago. "I was married at the time, helping my husband get his business started. I was in a job that I didn't like just because we needed a secure foundation. We lived in the suburbs and had the home and the whole nine yards and we needed a certain amount of income. I had started at the bottom as a sales clerk with the May Company in St. Louis, Missouri, and worked my way up the ladder to become a buyer.

Meg Biddle
Illustrator

"That training was really good for me, but I just got really tired of the egos and the struggles, all the paper-pushing. I wanted something better for myself. I was not interested in moving up any further within the corporate structure. I had reached buyer level — it had taken ten years to get there — but I took a look at the position the next step up from buyer and at the individual in that position — how they operated and the stress they were under and said, 'Why would I want to work any harder and go any further in the corporate structure if this is what I have to look forward to?'

"Finally it came to the point where I said, 'Enough is enough. I've had it.' I gave two weeks notice at my job and was gone. I didn't know exactly what I wanted to do, but I did know I wanted to get out and sell. I wanted to be part of the world instead of stuck behind a desk and on the telephone dealing with the egos.

"At first I was looking for something sort of mindless. Because I'd come from a corporate background, I didn't want to waste my time and energy with a company I knew I didn't intend to stay with." Ordinarily, finding such a job wouldn't be hard, but Patrish's background proved to be a problem. She was clearly overqualified. "I even tried getting a waitress job, but no one wanted to hire me because of my background. They could see that it was only a matter of time before I would be gone. So I was really confused and upset. Finally, I responded to a 'Me? Shine Shoes?' ad in the newspaper."

Patrish remembers the day vividly; already she was vigorously selling herself. "I went down to this truck stop dressed up in what my concept of what a shoe shine valet should look like. I wore a pair of black guacho pants and a shined-up pair of black boots — I had a little white top on — and of course I got there early. I walked over to where the appointment was supposed to be and found that what I had thought was going to be a private interview was actually a group interview. There was already a crowd of women there and I had come in on the end. After about ten minutes this guy with a big Stetson hat and exotic leather boots says, 'Well, alright, if you're interested, fill out this application.'" Patrish, sitting next to him, started to protest. She said, "I was under the impression that I was going to have an interview. Where *are* those stands?" The Stetson hat looked at her, pointed a fat finger and said, "You're management potential. You come back tomorrow."

Patrish recalls that she went home and thought about it that night. Having nothing really to lose, she decided she might as well hear the fellow's pitch. She learned that the man represented a national shoe shine company which had opened a single stand at the city's annual stock show. The idea was to open several more stands in order to make the effort profitable. But Patrish had bigger ideas. "I came up with a proposal. I took him around the city and showed him what I had in mind. I said 'This is what I want and this is what I'll do for you.' So they took me on and we opened 13 stands in 13 weeks."

Patrish soon began to chafe at some of the company's policies, however. Faced with the prospect of looking for a new job, she chose instead to strike out on her own. After six months of on-the-job training, she left the company to launch her own shoe shine business.

"I didn't know exactly where to start, so while I was having my stands built I went out to the Air Force base. I just walked right out there with my little portable kit and said, 'Here I am! I'd like to shine shoes on your air force base; who do I see?' I shined some colonel's shoes and he fell in love with me. They took pictures of me and put it in their paper and that turned out to be my first account.

"Patrish opened five of her own stands that first year. "Being an owner/operator, I would go in and open a location and get it going, then hire someone to operate the stand." After a time, however, keeping track of the operators, collecting lease fees and commissions, proved too much of a time and energy drain and Patrish divested herself of the stands, shifting her focus to her own in-home service and to consulting and training for large companies. Her goal is to restore the high standards of the valet profession "that have been lost in the shuffle."

At the three-year mark, Patrish finds great satisfaction in her work. "I'm very proud of what I've done with my business, the growing process and the things I've learned." The challenge of creating a career for herself, of making an idea work, has been immensely self-affirming. "I'm in the driver's seat," she smiles.

Opting Out of Company Politics

Women and minorities often find that self-employment brings freedom from a particularly nasty form of company dominion: on-the-job discrimination. Betsy Morscher describes the work environment she left. "I was in a corporation that didn't want women, hired them only because they were forced to by the Equal Opportunity Act. In an organization of 3,700, there were only five women in executive positions and my boss, a former West Point grad who thought women could do nothing right except make babies, made it unmercifully difficult for all of us. Things that men were able to do and took for granted were made three times harder for women. If I wanted to go to a seminar that related to my particular area of responsibility, I would have to not only fill out a form, I would have to go before a personal reviewing board to plead my case. I would have to write out a proposal about what kind of benefits I would get from the seminar, how long I anticipated being gone from the company and how I expected this to affect my job performance. Whereas a man would catch the boss in the hall and say 'Hey, John, I've got this seminar I want to go to.' John would say 'Sure, Pete. Just let me know how much money you need and we'll get you going there.' I saw it happen time after time."

Discrimination isn't the only type of company politics you'll avoid by becoming your own boss. One problem for self-starting entrepreneurial types is that they often work too hard, give too much to their jobs. Managers are often threatened and, inevitably, someone becomes dissatisfied. Working alone, or at least for yourself, eliminates the kind of constraining personal dynamics that can drive an achievement or goal-oriented person crazy. "In your own business," remarks Kathe MacLaren, "you only have yourself to blame. Each situation is a learning experience. You gain confidence, you learn what works, and ultimately, you have only yourself and your partner to answer to. You don't have to jump through hoops for someone else's ego.

"You also don't have people being jealous. When I was working in an office, the secretary, because I was older and more educated than she, was horribly jealous of me. She thought I was going to take her job."

Reflecting on this, Pauli Wanderer says "I guess I'm generally over-conscientious. I created a lot of pressure for myself trying to gain the approval of others. Working for myself somehow relieved me of that burden. I feel more relaxed working for myself, knowing that nobody's going to climb all over me for making a mistake."

Not only is it uncomfortable for most people to work under the kind of pressure Pauli describes, it's also counter-productive. As corporate psychologist Layne Longfellow puts it, "Stress is inversely proportional to productivity; as stress rises, productivity drops." Furthermore, stress levels are highest first, among laborers and next, among secretaries; contrary to popular thought, "hotshot executives come much further down the list," says Longfellow. He believes that the issue, once again, is one of control.

"One of the major problems with laborers and secretaries is the feeling of powerlessness. Secretaries typically feel that other people are in control of their lives." While people at the high end of the occupational scale may be under terrific pressure, usually there is the compensating sense of having chosen one's lifestyle, of being in control.

THE ENTREPRENEURIAL MOTHER:
AN OASIS OF CONTROL

At a recent seminar for women thinking of starting their own home-based businesses, it was noted that over 60 percent of all women with children work outside the home. "Why is that?" the presenter asked the group. A mother in the back drew appreciative laughter when she wearily answered, "Because they have children." Many women have found the combined chores of homemaking and parenting a formidable challenge to both stamina and self-esteem: so many demands; so comparatively few immediate, tangible rewards. Often, even a part-time job can help.

Janna Haynie, mother of three daughters between 18 months and five years old, feels she went into parenting fairly well prepared. "I wasn't 18 and starry-eyed," she says. "I realized when I went into this that there would be a drastic change, but it's hard to anticipate just how much of a change it will be." One major complication has been her husband's work. Now in his lat year of medical training as an internist, the time demands are almost unbelievable. Over a hundred hours a week, reports Janna, and those highly unpredictable. "We really like to have dinner together, to spend every evening together as a family, but he can be home anywhere from six in the evening to not at all, and we don't ever know." With her husband's work schedule and her children's school and activity schedules, it is Janna who must remain flexible. As with many young mothers, control is consequently important.

"I talk a lot about control but when you're in a situation where you have very small children and a husband in a very demanding career, the only person who loses control, who has to make all the accomodations for everyone in the family, is me. That can be a real drain."

A former teacher, Janna found that tutoring in her own home was a way of bringing a much-needed infusion of control into her life. "I set the pace. I decide how much we're going to get accomplished. I can organize it and see results. When your life is being controlled by so many elements that you lack power over, it's really nice to get into a situation where with your preparation and your students' eagerness and willingness to work, you can really move ahead. It does wonders for your self-image; it sort of keeps the balance you otherwise might not have.

"I don't regret my choice at all," says Janna. "On the other hand, it's nice to have something that keeps you current in your field and to be working at something you enjoy. It's probably more beneficial to me than anybody I tutor because it's that one area in my life where there's a lot of feedback, a lot of interaction, and especially a chance to be in control and have things work out the way they're supposed to."

CONTROL OVER DAILY LIFESTYLE

Sometimes it's the smaller areas of discretion that bring the most gratification. As Blanche Bennett illustrates, "I love doing things when I want to instead of having a clock telling me what to do. My shop is right in my garage so when I get up in the morning, if I want to go up in my shop and work I do, and if I don't, well, I have an 'open' and 'closed' sign on the lawn. People call me if they want to come and stop by. It's like being a free person.

"You decide how you want to spend your time," says Ralph Jackson. "If I want to work at home for two hours and then go jogging before I go to work, nobody's going to hassle me about that." Jackson adds that one direct benefit of being able to organize his own schedule is a boost in productivity. "I guess my favorite part of the day would have to be the early morning. Usually I get up very early, come down and study the scriptures, read and organize for the day, write my journal, then work on whatever other things I need to do. If I can get up at five or five-thirty and work for a couple or three hours, I probably get more done than I do in twice the time later in the day. It's quiet, uninterrupted, and physically and emotionally I'm fresh."

KEEPING YOUR EYE ON THE BALL

"There's paying rent, then there's your career," says Meg Biddle. "Eventually I will be sitting in my studio on the coast of California — that's the ball that I have to keep my eye on. Still, sometimes you get concerned about paying the bills, so you'll do some brochures or a restaurant menu to make a little money, and before you know it, you start losing track of the stuff that you're really good at, the things that say, 'It's Me.' When that happens," warns Meg, "it's time to rewite your job description."

Rewriting your job description may be impossible in a corporation where your personal development is not likely to be a company priority. As many a vice president has sadly found out, people are for the most part interchangeable; as soon as your personal goals begin to interfere with established routines you find yourself at odds with the powers that be. No

Patrish Wiggens
The Velvet Touch

hard feelings; it's the nature of companies large and small, and it will probably be the same when your own company becomes large enough to hire significant numbers of employees. The trick is to recognize this and instead of wasting energy and talent chafing in the harness, simply transfer yourself into a position where you *are* the powers that be.

Personal Contact:
The Key Ingredient

"I've been searching for the reason I'm so happy doing this and I really don't know why," says Richard Schwartz. "It has to do with the fulfillment you get when you can supply people with at least part of what they need. It has to do with the way that everybody you encounter teaches you something, gives you something, and you give back to them. That giving back and forth is a great experience. No matter what happens with this, just as long as the people are there, I'm happy."

It's not surprising that personal contact is ranked high on the list of motivations for self-employed baby-boomers. Theirs, after all, is the generation of the Peace Corps, the civil rights movement, Head Start, the Concert for Bangladesh. Rejecting what they considered to be the misguided values of big business, millions opted instead for the helping professions. Now, with shrinking government budgets for social programs, we see teachers working as computer salesmen, social workers tending bar — and a rising tide of service-minded people starting ventures in which they can operate on a more human level.

With the goal of providing services that both meet needs and contribute to the quality of life, many create jobs deliberately centered around personal interaction. As Richard Schwartz explains, people and relationships are the bottom line; customer appreciation, even friendship, are the big payoffs.

BROOKE DURLAND: THE ADVENTURE NETWORK

"People are paying so much more attention to vacations these days. There's a lot more stress, hence, lots more interest in really having escapes rather than just hanging out on a three-day weekend going 'Gee, what do we do?' People don't just throw things in the car and go; even for two or three days they seem to be willing to spend a lot of time and money planning." Brooke Durland explains the burgeoning interest in wilderness vacations that has prompted her and her husband Eric to form The Adventure Network, a clearinghouse for outfitters.

Brooke Durland
Colorado Adventure Network

In the fifties the ideal vacation was a stay at a luxurious resort. Why the current interest in wilderness trips? What's happening? "People have done the slickness," replies Brooke. "They've done the hot spots, the centers in Hawaii, Florida, the windjammer cruises. They want something that's different. They want to challenge themselves. They want that sense of accomplishment, that sense of 'I didn't think I could do it, but by golly, I did it!' and they can't get it sitting on the beach in Miami.

"The other reality is that all the baby boomers are having kids. Having waited longer to have children, they already had established hobbies and lifestyles that included vacations and sports — cross-country skiing, backpacking, cycling. We don't want to stop doing those things and that usually means taking the kids along. The reality is that it's very hard to do it with kids. Eric and I have struggled with little kids on trips so we're very realistic. If a customer asks 'can we do it with an eight-year-old?' we pretty much know what they can and can't do. We can steer them toward something that will be positive for everybody instead of a very expensive disaster.

"Another factor that brings people to us is discretionary money. All the people who in their twenties were doing all those activities are now in their thirties and now have kids and other financial commitments. We make it easier for those people.

"You can't overestimate the value of the personal contact with someone who knows what the trips are like, what to expect," continues Brooke. "For example, a woman might call and say, 'I'm traveling alone and I want to come out. I've got two weeks; what can I do?' Last year I signed up two women and one ended up going on a llama trip for part of the time, then on to a rafting trip down in Green River, Utah. When you really need to talk to someone who knows the details — I mean a travel agent isn't going to know what it's like, and if you call the llama packer he won't know anything about the raft trip — our kind of personal contact is very helpful."

Challenge is a big part of the adventure trips, Brooke says. "There's an emotional high you can't get from a Las Vegas trip. It brings back an element of excitement and personal challenge. People max out on the experience. Especially on the canoe trips, people don't expect that they can make it. You are so alone; there are no traffic lights; money means nothing. Toilet paper or a fishing lure is *very* valuable but money? Nooo! The only concerns are 'Where am I going to camp?' 'Is the wood going to be dry?' 'Am I going to find a flat place for my sleeping bag?' The only demands are very basic, elemental ones."

Describing her first canoe trip, the one on which she both met Eric and became a confirmed devotee, Brooke says, "It was the dynamic of a group effort: Because none of us could have done it alone, we got to know each other so well. In fact, there were 20 people and a couple of relationships came from that two weeks. Nothing occurred on the trip — nobody dared tip the balance by being anything other than platonic — but afterward people said,

'You know, I really knew you as a person then.' You knew them when they were tired and grubby and wet and muddy, as well as sunning on the rocks on a good afternoon. Those bonds and friendships are real motivators. Plus, everyone can really shine in a team effort. There are strengths that you wouldn't find out about at a cocktail party. And for women, it can be a wonderful discovery of their own capacities because on a canoe trip, it's not so much strength as endurance that's important."

Brooke notes that even after ten years of leading wilderness excursions, the thrill of watching the personal transformations is undiminished; it's as if being a catalyst in the process is an integral part of her own job satisfaction.

"It really is. Often I'll write something in our brochure like 'It will make memories that will last all winter,' and that's true — it's almost intoxicating. You come away thinking, 'I want to do it again.' The most satisfying thing for me is realizing that I am helping people fulfill their dreams."

Brooke is a perfect example of the service-minded entrepreneur. In her mid-thirties, she's worked as a public school psychologist for several years, and continues to counsel three days a week. The network is just a different mode of promoting emotional health.

EMILY HUNTER: THE BRIAR ROSE INN

If you can't change the world, try changing a little piece of it might be Emily Hunter's work philosophy. In an increasingly cold and anonymous society, her brain child, the Briar Rose Inn, is a bit of home.

"Bed and breakfast is not a new idea," says Hunter. "There have been inns in existence since the 1400s, the idea being that when people leave their home turf they're still human beings and they still have certain needs." Hunter says the operating philosophy behind the Briar Rose Inn, a sprawling, one-story Victorian home, is that people's needs go beyond food and shelter, that personal attention and concern, a sense of connectedness, is important to the traveler.

"In the town I grew up in — Urbana, Virginia — right down the street was Miss Maude's Guest House. There was also the commercial hotel downtown on the corner of Main, where all the traveling salesmen stayed, but gentlemen and ladies, the relatives of the people in town, all stayed at Miss Maude's."

Recalling the gradual disappearance of places like Miss Maude's, Emily explains that "with the advent of the automobile, our society became much more mobile and there was a lot less trust. People needed the confidence of an

Emily Hunter
Briar Rose Inn

expected motel room; they got very enamored with the idea of efficiency and anonymity — you drive up and somebody hands you a key over a counter; you don't look at them, they don't look at you. The whole idea of 'host' disappeared and with it went the inns."

But the last five years has seen a tremendous resurgence of small inns; California alone boasts more than five hundred. "That's the nature of the cultural pendulum," says Emily. "It's just swinging back now. I think people are exploring what it is to be human, looking for ways in which they can become more related. The inn is just a place where people can reaffirm something.

"It doesn't take much to help foster that feeling of relatedness," she says. "I like to think that people feel their needs have been anticipated, that there's some respect for them as human beings. I mean, people are so grateful for the slightest considerations — a simple good morning, their beds being turned down, a chocolate on the pillow. Maybe they don't even eat candy — haven't for 30 years — it doesn't matter. Somehow a gesture of recognition's been made in their direction. It's people's appreciation that's actually the inspiration for this place."

How do travelers find the Briar Rose? "We're in eight or nine directories, but we rely a lot on local word of mouth and we do enjoy a nice local reputation. I've tried to figure out who comes here and why and I've found that we get all kinds of people: the traveling salesmen, the corporate execs, the mother-in-law from down the street, university students' parents. The thing they all have in common is an awareness and concern for their personal environment.

"People don't know what they're getting into when they come here for the first time. There's no Best Western sign out there, no AAA, and they must be thinking, 'What *is* this, for heaven's sake?' But they are really looking for something that will feed them in a certain way so they're willing to go for a little adventure. Our lives are so permeated by media, some people are consciously looking for something that is distinctively *non*-media. And again, there's the concern for relatedness. You don't have the neighborhood you once had. You move from city to city. Your famly lives on one coast, you live on the other. Your children are somewhere else. You live in a condominium and you don't even know the person who lives next to you. You're very lucky if you have a close circle of supportive friends." It's plain that everything about the Briar Rose has been calculated to restore a feeling of home.

It's the Little Things

When meeting Emily Hunter for the first time in the setting of the inn, she seems very much at home. Tall, soft-voiced, with long dark hair pulled up in a loose chignon, she seems the embodiment of the gracious Southern hostess. "This has not always been my lifestyle, believe me," she says. At 42, Emily cheerfully describes herself as "the proverbial aging hippie. I've lived in a three-room log cabin in Wyoming, on a sailboat, in an old farmhouse in Mendicino. But when I really wanted to think about an environment that meant home and comfort to me, I thought about the home I grew up in, about my grandmother's house at the end of the lane. I remembered how I felt in both of those homes and decided I wanted the inn to remind the traveler of his grandmother's home — or what he wished his grandmother's home was like."

Indeed, instead of boring white walls and woodgrained plastic furniture, the rooms of the Briar Rose seem to glow, their 90-year-old plaster walls painted a color called "Pancake," offset with stenciled trim of "Williamsburg

Blue." "These are the colors I grew up with," explains Emily. "I'm not a professional decorator and I didn't have the resources to hire one, so I just thought a lot about the house I grew up in."

There are eleven guest rooms in the inn, each one different. The towels hanging in the "Green Room" are not white but a deep juniper to match the down comforter on the bed. Satiny old furniture, gleaned from garage sales and Emily's house, is draped with hand-embroidered cloths. On a table by the window there rests a vase of fresh heather and two upturned crystal goblets. Everywhere there are baskets and sprays of dried flowers.

The guest who asks for a warm, quiet room might find herself on the second floor, far away from the bustle of the kitchen. The thermostat will have been nudged up far enough in advance that the room is already cozy when she arrives. In the closet there are padded satin hangers, and just in case she forgot her own, a large soft terry bathrobe. No "sanitation guaranteed" paper strips grace the toilet seats of the shared baths. The guest soaps are not paperwrapped Ivory but scented pastel shells. While the visitor is at dinner the bedcovers will have been turned down. The little things.

Breakfast is served from six to ten each morning. At five-thirty a.m. the linen-covered diningroom tables are already set with gold-rimmed china and crystal. Breakfast at the Briar Rose is "continental plus": hot coffee, black or herb teas, fresh-squeezed orange juice; croissants served with butter, marmalade or a homemade lemon curd; fruit yogurt garnished with bits of green apple.

At first, the homey atmosphere of the place is a little disconcerting to the seasoned commercial traveler, who is apt to spend the first day creeping around, muttering "excuse me" before getting the hang of things. "When you have a room you get the whole house," Emily explains. Guests are encouraged to wander about, to help themselves to the cookie jar in the kitchen, to generally make themselves at home.

Indicating the ancient grape vine gnarling itself against the window of the breakfast porch, Emily says, "This grape vine doesn't look like much now in February, but pretty soon it will start making these incredibly beautiful little pink nodules that open into beautiful pink leaves. They're pink for a week or two, then they start turning darker green and getting bigger and bigger until the whole thing is just a shady bower. Then it starts making grapes and by fall the whole place smells like Welch's grape juice. We have a little Italian man who lives across the street who's taken care of the grapes for years. He says as soon as the racoons hit the grapes, that means the sugar content is high enough and it's time to pick. He takes all the grapes in one day and makes wine and brings us back some.

From Visualization to Reality

A friend recollects that bringing the Briar Rose Inn into existence was no small undertaking. "Emily stood out there in the beat-up yard, fighting the rose bushes, looked at this ramshackle old house and said we're going to do this and we're going to do that and you could just visualize it." Much of the reason for the inn's success, Emily's friend believes, was her ability to explain to investors and contractors her vision of what the place would one day be.

What prompted Emily, a single mother of two, to take on such a project? "I was looking for a situation that would incorporate both lifestyle and livelihood, a way of being in the world and being able to take care of children and provide the things you need. At the time I was new in real estate and got caught by interest rates that were 18 and 19 percent for residential property. I couldn't make money. So I started thinking, 'If you can't make money with property and numbers, maybe you can make money with property and an idea.'" Before Emily bought the house that was to become the Briar Rose, it had been "just an old rundown house where two very nice old people had lived for 40 years." The house had been bought by developers who planned to raze it and build — who knows? maybe an office or apartment building — but they too got caught by the interest rates and had to put it on the market.

What did it take to make the transformation from ramshackle old house to charming Victorian inn? "Move mountains! We had to bring it up to code, rewire, change the plumbing and the heating, move walls around. We had to build on more rooms to make it profitable to operate. All this took just over three months." Even with help, the restoration was a prodigious task.

Although the Briar Rose is really Emily's operation, it would be impossible to run without help. The place seems filled with amiable helpers. "We have eight people on the payroll, 24 hours a day, 365 days a year. People work in shifts and everybody does everything. There is naturally a lot of maid work and housekeeping but there is no 'maid,'" says Emily. "Each person answers the phone, takes care of the guests, takes care of emergencies. They get the praise, the problems. They take care of food, money. I feel that whoever's here is the host or hostess. There are a lot of things that need to be done away from the property when you're promoting a business. I'm here sporadically throughout the day. I don't want somebody with jogging shorts and a johnny mop in their hands kind of walking around saying 'I don't know.'

"We all knew that it was a gamble — I've worked very hard doing it and it wouldn't have happened the way it's happened without me and I know that. Part of the challenge is to try and make it what you originally envisioned — and the vision is always expanding. On the one hand, it's tyranny; on the other it's motivation and creativity. I want to have visualized something and been right about it. That's the ongoing challenge for me. Every day. Always."

People, People

If realizing her vision is Emily's major challenge, her greatest sense of fulfillment comes from observing the salutory effects of the Briar Rose on the people who come and stay. Emily notes that she has met some ordinary people who become extraordinary in this particular setting. "Because it's a human habitat, people do the things humans do and things happen to them. Lovers reconcile, marriages break apart.

"We had some outrageous Australians stay here for ten days. One of them, a man about 60, would appear for breakfast late every morning because he had to do a lot of business on the telephone in the middle of the night because of the time difference. He would come down to breakfast in his Playboy nightshirt and ski jacket, barefoot, with his little glasses down on his nose and a little hat that his wife knit to keep his bald head warm. And he'd be smoking a pipe that blew sparks. Every morning for ten mornings Roger Clark came down for breakfast that way.

"He had everybody in stitches. I mean people were sitting around the diningroom in their suits and here comes Roger, talking a mile a minute. 'Top of the morning to you, ladies and gentlemen!' When he left he sent us a sterling silver tea strainer. 'The next time I come,' he said, 'I don't want to have to read my fortune in the bottom of my tea cup!'

"We've actually had some rock bands stay here and it's been really nice. We had Chris Hillman's (The Birds, Flying Burrito Brothers) band stay here. The person who booked them here said they were really tired and had begged him to find some place that was quiet and nice. They really liked it and we loved having them. They would sit outside in the yard with their banjos and guitars and practice. The whole place was sort of permeated with this rock/bluegrass music. Ironically, when they were here we also had a delegation of five Chinese and a luncheon for the

University Women. It was a real active and diverse group and we all had a wonderful time."

A WIDENING CIRCLE OF FRIENDSHIPS: CHARLOTTE ELICH-McCALL

"I think for me — and this is typical of a lot of women in business — we're guilty of self-sabotaging behavior," remarks writer Betsy Morscher. "We know that one of the prices of moving too quickly is leaving behind friends and allies. It can be very lonely." True, but on the other hand, many people find that the few friendships they lose are replaced by many more new ones. Charlotte Elich-McCall, for example, is amazed at the number and variety of worthwhile new relationships she's gained since going into business.

"I've always said that the reason I got into this was I was a weaver and I like to do that," says Charlotte, "but the human contact is very important. I like the diversity of the people who come in. I don't think I would be happy working in an office and only having a little office group around me. And I love working with people. I love winding off yarn and helping them decide what they want and answering questions on the phone, trying to get people to come here.

"I would definitely say that the business has made me more out-going. I've always been — and still am — labeled shy, except that you can't really be that shy when you have to be with the public all the time. You can't hang out in the back room because you're afraid to talk to people."

One nice result, she says, is a growing circle of friends. "I've made more friends — especially female friends — since I opened the business than I've had in my whole life. Maybe because the people who come in here have the same interests as me. We have that connection already that we are all craftspeople." Working with craftspeople, Charlotte feels, has spared her some of the headaches normally thought to be inevitable. "I think I have wonderful customers. One example is that in seven years of business I've had only one bad check that I couldn't collect on. This creative kind of clientele seems to be more honest."

THE HELPING MENTALITY

Brooke Durland, Emily Hunter and Charlotte Elich-McCall approach business with an emphasis on personal contact. Other entrepreneurs share this approach with an added emphasis on lending a helping hand.

"A Very Warm Feeling": Blanche Bennett

"I was at the post office 37 years; 31 as a postal clerk and then the last 6 years I was postmaster. I think what bothered me most was I just went to work, opened that window, sorted that mail, sold those stamps — I was a servant. They expected me to be there at that window, expected those reports to be there on time. I was a number, that's all I was. They didn't know me personally — I was just a machine." Blanche Bennett's recollections of her years as a civil servant leave little question about why she is "so thankful I decided to retire," especially when she describes her new way of life.

In the little Massachusetts town of Ashley Falls, where the population hovers around 700, it would seem the business opportunities for a retired 60-year-old woman would be somewhat limited. Be that as it may, Blanche — or Aunty Bea, as her nieghbors have called her for years, has found a perfect niche for herself as combination shopowner/teacher/listening ear. "Aunty Bea's Shoppe," ensconced in her own converted garage, is filled with handmade crafts: Blanche's braided rugs, her sister Inez' knitted and crocheted clothing, and contributions from various friends. Given the size of her market, the little store has done remarkably well. Blanche notes that after her open house last June, she was swamped with orders and had to have three other women knitting around the clock to fill them all.

While she is unquestionably her own boss, ("I don't run the shop on an eight-to-five basis. I'm open when I'm here.") the label "entrepreneur" seems somehow not to fit. For Blanche, the business is not based on gross margins or accounts receivables or bottom lines, but on friendships and sharing, for, Blanche explains, while she enjoys selling, her real love is the small, informal classes where she teaches other women to make rugs.

"I've built good relationships with a lot of people. I always serve coffee and dessert after class, and I had a Christmas party for all the girls that have come so far. Each one brought the first rug she had made and we took pictures. They just seemed to love it. And the girls all brought me cookies and candies and a lovely floral arrangement. It gives me a very warm feeling that they enjoy me as a person, not just as a teacher.

"I put a lot of time and effort into my classes," Blanche says. "I don't expect to get all that back money-wise; it's just the pleasure of making all those girls happy. It gives them a night out away from the children. Some of them are divorced, unhappy. It's something to do with their time." Then chuckling, she adds, "And they sort of pour out their problems to me — I'm sort of a Dear Abby. I just have a good feeing about it all."

Sharing a Sense of Connectedness

Helping people is an important concern for antique dealer Pauli Wanderer, who says, "My background is in teaching and social work. Although I love antiques, I worry that I'm not in a helping profession. I'm in business to make money — that's always been sort of dirty in my book."

What about her contribution to people's lives? In an increasingly cold and alienating society, adding warmth and humanity to a person's environment can be a great service. "Yes. I really think that's what this great interest in country furniture is all about. People in cities are crazy for it because in a nameless Manhattan apartment building, they want that feeling of soft old quilts, of 'down home.'

"These things have a history built in. I met this older divorced woman who had lost all her possessions in the divorce settlement. She was very disoriented and lost for a while. When she came out here her son built her a country house of her own and I helped her furnish it with things I'd gathered from all over the country." Not just furnish her house, but also help her rebuild her sense of roots and connectedness she had lost. "Yes that's right. We've become friends now. She calls me and brings in her samples and I help her decide what to put with them. Or I'll have her over for a glass of wine and we'll talk."

One-to-One: Janna Haynie

Often men and women are drawn to the teaching profession because of the opportunities to help others meet their goals, only to find themselves so burdened with administrative duties that the student/teacher relationship is lost in policies and paperwork. Teacher Janna Haynie was delighted to find that tutoring in her home provided a perfect setting for one-to-one helping, something she feels is even more satisfying than the paycheck.

"You talk about self-esteem — adults with reading problems also generally have some kind of self-esteem problem, because if you've reached a certain stage in your life and your skills are deficient, you're very aware of it. Seeing them gain self-esteem in addition to getting actual reading skills is as important to me as my own success.

"I worked with one man who was a mechanic and a very good one, but he was struggling because he couldn't complete the paperwork he needed to do to run his business. He also wanted to teach in a vocational school but he had a great sense of fear because he knew he didn't have the reading skills that most of his students would have. As I worked with him he gained a lot of self-confidence. He learned how to quit trying to cover up for the fact that he couldn't read and actually get some skills. That was really satisfying.

"I think it's good for the students to have that relationship with the tutor. In fact, the one-to-one relationship is probably as important to their success as overcoming the program itself. I think adult non-readers often have a whole set of insecurities and problems in addition to needing skill work and they sort of unfold once they know how to read."

Lending a Hand

As Brian Finn pointed out, owning your own business means having both the ability and the authority to use knowledge and influence to help those you'd like to help. While altruism might seem to run counter to the image of the "born salesman," Thelton Skipper and Patrish Wiggens — two self-described hustlers — count the sense of having helped others one of their most gratifying rewards.

"I love to feel that I can help people. I get a joy and a sense of accomplishment out of that even without the money. If I can help you as a client, see you quit paying so much in taxes, see you make more money — if I can make you happy then I'm happy." Over the years, Skip has worked on a gratis basis with several clients, widows and elderly women, helping them arrange their affairs, in some cases managing rental properties, simply for the satisfaction of helping out.

"I'm a people person," states Patrish Wiggens, by way of explaining what it is she hopes to accomplish through her business. "Because of the way I operate, every individual who comes to me is a better person when they leave and I am better for having known them. My number-one priority is that the customer has my undivided attention for ten minutes. He has the opportunity to just relax and enjoy.

"I've met so many people from all walks of life and from all parts of the country; when you add up the good things you learn from each individual, you get closer to your own goals."

One of Patrish's most important goals is, in her own way, to make a positive impact on the world. Using the vehicle of an engaging service business that often attracts media attention, she brought community notice to several benevolent organizations, including the Volunteers of America. "One holiday season I shined shoes for dollars and raised over $200 for charity in one weekend. When you work with the less fortunate, teaching and trying to make the world a better place, you receive more in return."

A PERPETUAL LEARNING EXPERIENCE

"There is no end to this business I have," says used and rare book dealer Richard Schwartz. "There's something new every day. It's wonderful if you don't mind always being a student. I'm constantly learning something, whether it's about the weather and different types of plows from the best organic farmer in the state, or whatever — I'm always learning and that, in itself, is an energizing process.

"One thing that has come to me, along with the thrill of meeting and learning things from people, is that I have developed an expertise that amazes me. I don't really know I have it until I start talking with a friend — and it's come inadvertently from this constant give and take with customers much more than from straight research. It literally amazes me, when I start talking with someone, just how much I know." He laughs. "That's a wonderful thing to experience for a guy who never thought he'd be an expert on anything."

Many find that striking out on their own brings an education, not only in business, but also in human nature. As one new employer notes, part of being the boss entails making the most of employees' talents, learning to lead a team. Becoming the captain stretches communication skills, the ability to listen and empathize. And frequently, there is the humbling lesson that you can't do it alone.

"Being around so many different people has a way of tearing down stereotypes," comments Pauli Wanderer. "Having been in the academic world for so long, it's interesting that people with no education at all, who might speak very poor English, might collect the most sophisticated items and be very knowledgeable about them. They may have no education but collect the creme de la creme Tiffany glass and *know* that glass. The same goes for dealers," Pauli adds. "There are a lot of knowledgeable dealers with no formal education."

For magazine publisher Garrett Giann, learning to work with employees has been a crucial part of his business education. Working for yourself, Giann says, "you avoid a lot of concern about the politics of getting ahead: 'Did I say the right thing to him? Am I too hard-working? Does he think I'm after his job?' You don't have to worry about that when you're the head honcho. What you do have to worry about is things like how well you listen to employees when they're upset. If you don't listen or deal with it diplomatically enough you might alienate them and you can lose that way, too.

"I think the whole reason one would want to be in business, aside from the demands of making money, is to derive some satisfaction out of the human contacts," reflects Giann. "You have to derive some satisfaction, some joy from your dealings with other people in business — there's got to be a handshake, a slap on the back, a thank you. It can't be just beating everybody to death trying to see who can win and get the best deal — there's got to be some respect, some camaraderie."

Well put.

Marketing

"If you don't have a customer you don't have a business."
Marlene Ospina, President
Women Business Owner's Association

Marketing, the basic challenge of all businesses, begins at the conceptual stage with a thorough study of the business climate in your area. Before you apply for a loan, before you sign a lease — even before you fill out your five-year business plan — you must know who your customers are and what their needs and buying habits are. Publisher and seminar producer Howard L. Shenson states, "Bad marketers begin with a product or a service and ask the question, 'How can I sell it?' Good marketers start with the market and say, 'What does the market want?' and then design the product or service to fit the marketplace." When counseling the person looking for a business opportunity, Marlene Ospina takes Shenson's idea a step further. "I always tell people, 'Don't think in terms of what you love doing. Think instead of what you hate doing, then find a way to make it easier. Choose a product or a service that will solve a problem, fill a need."

The entrepreneurs in this chapter have built successful businesses not by doing things they hate, but by finding enjoyable ways to meet their customers' needs. For an example of starting with the market and designing a service to fit the market, consider Bill Felder's business.

"I love what I do," Bill Felder says of his work as a freelance chef and caterer. Although his schooling, experience and personality all make him ideally suited for the food business, the key to Bill's success is the way he has examined the market, appraised his own assets and come up with the two winning ideas that comprise his small catering service, "The Occasional Chef." He has directed his marketing efforts toward two specific groups: young urban professionals and the local film industry.

Joan Robey
Robey-Slabech Gallery

"We yuppie folk have developed our own market," Felder reflects. "If, as a working female professional, you're billing your time at $60 an hour, and your husband is a professional who's billing his time at $100 a hour, you can't justify coming home and cooking. So when all of a sudden you're giving a party for eight or ten of your nearest and dearest, what do you do? To take them to a restaurant's going to cost you $500."

The couple might be willing to entertain at home, of course, but as Bill points out, there is a problem. To nicely entertain at home you need to hire a caterer, but few caterers will cater a party for only ten or twelve, simply because the profits aren't great enough to cover fixed expenses. "So there's a void of anyone who's doing small stuff and doing it well. There are a lot of housewives who will come in and cook for you or serve for you, but I've got three tuxedos hanging upstairs and a lot of knowledge."

A lot of knowledge, indeed. "I grew up in this business," says Pittsburgh-born and bred Felder, whose family owned a neighborhood deli. "My grandfather gave me my first set of whites when I was five years old. I used to stand on a Canada Dry box in the back of the deli and run the slicer." After a stint in the Navy, Bill attended college and graduated with a degree in hotel and restaurant management. Later, he attended the Culinary Institute of America in New York. At 38, he looks back at some ten years in the field, during which time he managed several restaurants, worked for a catering business and taught cooking classes at a local gourmet foods store. Just before launching his own catering service, he held a position as chef and staff manager in a private executive home. "So my background is good," he says. "I've been exposed to all the right stuff, read all the right books."

Felder's biggest asset, however, just might be his gregarious personality. Irreverently funny, a showman of sorts, he's a natural for the kind of business in which clockwork efficiency must be tempered with an easy, gracious manner. Bill is an enthusiastic host. "The fun part is going out and talking with the people," he remarks. "If you don't have any contact with the customer you could just as easily be doing auto body work."

Felder's expertise not only earns him top dollar as a private chef, but often places him in glamorous company, as well. Heiresses and movie magnates are among his customers. "I had five couples take me to Aspen with them for two days. They wanted to ski and wanted to eat well and didn't want to be hassled with restaurants. I charge $425 per day, all expenses paid by the client, so I got $850 for two days' work." A good living, he admits, but he does work hard. "I did breakfast and they were on the slopes when the lifts opened. And I did a plush breakfast — Eggs Benedict, sausage and fried apples, fritters. When they came back about midday I served drinks and dips. Dinner at night. I was working all day."

INDENTIFYING A MARKET NICHE

Felder noticed that he had met a lot of local movie people over the years, and he began to investigate the possibilities of serving that market. He liked what he found. "Last year alone there was $12 million in movie money that came into the state — 48 commercials, three feature-length movies. There's not only twelve million bucks coming in from outside, there's also a bunch of local people doing commercials. In essence, over 200 days (last year) someone was in town shooting a movie, and no one was catering to those people."

Felder explains that on every shoot there is a sizeable crew, in addition to the actors, that requires at least one, if not three meals each day. While the meals have somehow been provided in the past, Felder had the idea that the service wasn't really adequate. What usually happened, he says, is that the production manager would call a friend who owns a restaurant, who would agree to bring over some sandwiches and coffee. "Or he'll call a social caterer and the lady shows up with scones and tea for breakfast. Now you think about movies and all you see is the pretty people — the cute little size eight actress and her co-stars — but that's only four people. The movie shoot has 15 to 30 people in the crew and most of them look like retired football players. They're big people — technicians, lighting people carrying around these big pieces of machinery. They get there at six o'clock in the morning and unload the truck and set the stuff up. All their equipment is rented and they're paying for it by the day or the hour; the director and production assistant are running around like crazy trying to get everything done in a hurry. When it comes time for lunch, they're tired. You need to give them 3,000 calories in 35 minutes.

"So my thought was, 'Let's put something together to take care of the movie industry.'" An additional thought was how neatly the two catering operations would fit together; while private parties are generally evening affairs, the movie shoots would provide additional daytime business.

TESTING THE WATER

Financial planner Thelton Skipper is glad to share tips with the newcomer. The most common mistake, in his opinion, is "jumping into self-employment without having done enough research beforehand." With all Bill Felder's training and experience in the food business, he still spent months doing his own feasibility study. He looked carefully at the market in which he had worked for years; he asked knowledgeable friends for advice; he gathered financial data from the state movie council and found out who the production managers were. It was only after he was certain there was a niche he could fill that he began structuring his new business. No one, says Thelton Skipper, should even think of going into a new venture without first doing some investigation to find out basic facts about the market. For example:

- What is the population in your area? Could your business draw from surrounding communities?

- What are the incomes of your potential customers? What age groups are predominant?

- What are the households like? Do students comprise a large portion of the population? Military people? Young professional couples? How many households include children? How many people are retired?

- What are the buying habits of your potential customers? Do most people entertain at home or go to restaurants? Do they travel or spend vacations at home?

- When thinking of a new business, check to see how many similar ones there already are in your area. If there are too many, you may find that the competition is too strong unless you have something truly unique to offer. If there are no others, it could be because there is no market for your idea or the market is currently undeveloped.

Mention market research to prospective entrepreneurs, anxious to get started on their business ideas, and you're likely to hear two objections: "I can't waste time on research," and "I can't afford it." The first objection is so self-evidently illogical that no argument is necessary. As for the second objection, while cost may be a legitimate concern, the fact is you can't afford *not* to research your market. Happily, the process needn't be elaborate or expensive — in fact, says Skipper, you can probably find everything you need to know right in your own public library.

THE NEED FOR PATIENCE AND DETERMINATION

Occasionally a person will see great potential for a given product or service but will also recognize that customer tastes or buying habits currently wouldn't justify the business. It's known that certain states — California and Florida, for example — are "bellweather" states, while other areas are much slower to embrace new trends. Being ahead of one's time doesn't necessarily mean an idea won't work; it might only mean that a little patience is required until the local market evolves. Gallery owner Joan Markowitz firmly believes that patience was a major factor that enabled her to successfully bring her business along. What began as a tiny storefront stocked with functional ceramics — "cups and mugs" — is now a thriving gallery offering sophisticated fine art and contemporary crafts. But the transformation took time. "We've often acknowledged that the clientele had to be developed," says Joan. "If we had started out five years ago with the inventory we have now, we would have gone out of business."

"INTERSUPPLIFICATION"

"I think it's imperative that you take some time to develop contacts," says Bill Felder. "The one big advantage of working for other people is that I got to know a lot of their customers and friends. I know the people who are interested in (having small dinners catered). I know probably 100 people well enough to walk into their office and shake hands. Each of those people would probably try me once, and they in turn will each give me two or three referrals.

"As for the movie shoots, my most helpful contact has been a lady who is a freelance production manager. She works probably 150 to 200 days a year. I met her through a friend of mine, a local movie producer. When he was first starting in the business he used to come into the restaurant I managed and write scripts at the counter."

Cartoonist Meg Biddle has escaped much of the hardship associated with paying one's dues in the arts, a fact she attributes to having moved in business circles several years before pursuing her career as a humorist. "There were some lean times," she recalls, "but not the way I hear a lot of people go through. I think my business background really helped me. I had figured out how to talk to clients and not be afraid of them. I knew a lot of people in the business community who gave me jobs. I know how to network and I do it as much as possible — I should say 'intersupplificate' — I'm so sick of using the word 'networking.'" Whatever you want to call it, it's an essential part of marketing.

SELLING TO MEET A NEED

To once more refer to Howard L. Shenson's advice, the idea is not to come up with a cartoon and then hope to sell it, but instead to create artwork (or any other product or service) to fill a need. Another thing to remember, says Meg, is that you can't just sit home in your studio waiting for jobs. Her suggestion: "Go to meetings you might not think would have anything to do with art work. I still have a great interest in business. I'm always curious about what's going on and I'm always trying to come up with suggestions here and there for my clients. If you stay in touch, somewhere down the line you can do something for them. You can solve a problem for them without their even asking. That's unsolicited stuff, but it works like a charm.

"It all started with [one man I knew] who's been my best client. We would meet each other and I would have some drawings I had just been working on with him in mind. I'd just come with my doodles and he'd say, 'Oh, this is perfect for. . . .' You know, if you get to know somebody and get to know their business needs, you know how to target them."

WINNING IN A COMPETITIVE MARKET

Competing for a share of the market can be especially difficult for the small businessperson when time as well as money is spread thin. The owner of a one- or two-person operation often simply lacks the manpower necessary to make repeated sales calls or to sustain the intensive personal contact required to develop and maintain accounts. For example, Kenneth Moyer, president of Moyer Texas Champagne Company, would like to expand his clientele by adding more restaurant accounts to his existing retail store trade. As always, there are obstacles to be overcome.

"It's easy to get in the door of a retail store," Moyer says. "All they have to do is push a few bottles aside and put yours right up there. But with a restaurant, unless you're on their wine list, they're not going to sell any of your wines." The problem, he continues, is that a restaurant customarily prints a new wine list only two or three times each year. If a producer wants his wine included on the list, he must be there at the time of the printing because otherwise his product will be edged out by the half dozen others being pushed by his competitors. As the sole representative of his company, Moyer simply can't be in all the right places at all the right times. "Because of the enormous amount of ground I have to cover across the state of Texas, I can't get into as many restaurants as I would like. You need salesmen out there. You take a big distributor like American Wine Distributors — he'll have maybe 12 salesmen in Houston alone, and two or three will do nothing but call on restaurants. A small business can't do that."

ALTERNATIVES TO BIG BUDGETS

Telephone Sales

One partial solution to the need for being in three places at once is to hone your telephone sales skills, says Joe Koch, who is the marketing force behind a highly successful husband-and-wife venture. The brass kaleidoscopes hand-crafted by his wife, Sheryl, are sold in fine stores in cities as far-flung as New York and Honolulu. "Most of our orders tend to be phone orders," explains Joe, "and when you have someone who's calling you long distance from San Francisco or New York to place an order for two of these and two of those, *that's* the time to sell. You say, 'Gee, we've just had a super response to the Tripod, and we have a new model, the Bath Scope, and it has just taken off.' Your customer's response is 'Oh — well, you'd better give me some of those also.' By the time you finish that phone conversation, somebody who was calling to make a $200 order ends up making a $500 order."

Relieving the Cost Burden Through Networking

In addition to the time crunch, many new entrepreneurs face the challenge of finding affordable advertising. Small budgets usually mean that television and radio ads are out of the question, and even less expensive options like direct mail and trade listings can be seriously limited. Some entrepreneurs have found that co-ops can open doors.

Brooke Durland and her husband, Eric, have organized and led canoe trips ever since they first met on a Canadian excursion. Over the years they have met many outfitters who, like themselves, love the camaraderie and the challenge of leading wilderness outings but don't particularly enjoy the marketing end of the business. Brooke tells how this shared need became the germ of a home-based business.

"We had an idea that we could become a clearinghouse for outfitters and do the marketing for them. People could call us and say, 'I've got three days after the conference and two days on my way to California and I don't know what I want to do. What can you recommend?' and we would put them in touch with the people in our network."

The Durlands started out by deciding what kinds of outings they would like to include — some of those available are horsepacking, dude ranches, ballooning, bicycling and kayaking — and then contacted other outfitters they knew. Brooke found many were anxious to join the network, having themselves grappled with the economics of making trips profitable. "You can have four people and just break even," explains Brooke, "but if you can just get that fifth person you can show a profit." The clearinghouse idea would provide a better chance for signing that fifth person than each outfitter would have on his own.

Actually, The Adventure Network has proved to be a good deal for both the outfitters and their customers. The benefit to a vacationer is that there is less chance of a mismatch since Brooke knows each outfitter and is very familiar with the kind of trip he offers. One network member, for example, specializes in trips for women over 30. Brooke can even advise a family as to whether a trip would be appropriate for children.

Another advantage to both customer and outfitter is that Brooke is often able to make connections that would otherwise be missed. "A lot of our people are in the hinterlands and are difficult to reach. Like our llama packer — you can only get him at meal times, so unless you can talk to someone in the office who may or may not know a lot of the details, a phone call is a little tricky." With Brooke acting as go-between, the outfitter doesn't lose those customers.

The biggest advantage to networking, however, is that it lessens the advertising burden for each business. Each outfitter is listed in a printed brochure and contacts are shared. Although outfitters do pay a small commission, there is no initial fee and no membershp dues. The outfitters pay only when customers are booked. By pooling their resources, participants have been able to afford booths in major trade shows, too. "We went to two big shows last year," says Brooke, "one in Denver and one in Dallas. Booth space was $800. We wanted the exposure but there was no way we could afford that, so I called all our people and said, 'Look, if you'd like to throw in $100, you can come yourself and if you get any signups, its no commission to us.' At the Dallas show, the llama packer paid only a $50 booth fee and got three direct signups from brochures. So there are some advantages to a co-operative venture."

Highly Targeted Advertising

Experienced business owners recommend being very selective in using your advertising dollars; the best method, they say, is to find out who your customers are and then spend your ad money to target those people as specifically as possible. When Bill Felder decided to send printed flyers announcing the opening of his new movie-catering service, for example, he carefully narrowed his target group. He felt that a printing of only 200 flyers would be ample for reaching all the local industry people as well as the "seven or eight national ad agency people who handle this area. That's all there is." As you can imagine, Felder's costs for his direct mail campaign were extremely low.

The same targeted approach can be applied to other businesses and it is particularly effective in small communities where a business owner might have a nodding acquaintance with a good number of his neighbors. Cherry

Silver, who owns a bookstore in Moses Lake, Washington (population 12,000) says "I've done a little experimenting with advertising — ads in the local paper, ads in shoppers and small weeklies in outlying towns, but the best success I've had has been with a direct mailer to the people in our area that I know are interested in the books I carry. I have a mailing list of about 400 people that I'm expanding all the time."

Savings Tip: Joe Koch recommends using a brochure with pockets for inserts. That way, as your product line and prices change, you can keep the more expensive outer folder and just replace the sheets inside.

THE IMPORTANCE OF ATTITUDE

"If you have any self-doubts when you go in to sell . . . it shows all over your face like you're wearing a poster."
                                                                    Leslie Goodwin

First, last and always, the test of the entrepreneur will be one of salesmanship — selling his idea to his backers, selling his product or service to his customers, and above all, selling himself to everybody. Moreover, for most of us, that test of salesmanship will be the greatest continuing challenge we'll encounter, for the act of selling uncovers some of our worst fears and insecurities and forces us to put not only our ideas but our very selves on the line. In selling, attitude is everything.

Whether your business is well-established or just starting up, there is a perpetual need for selling and re-selling the customer. It may be that you want him to continue buying the same thing; in any case, one of the most powerful influences will be your attitude toward yourself and your product or service. Business directories publisher Leslie Goodwin says "I'm a real firm believer in positivism. A positive attitude is something that will give anyone an edge in competing. The minute you think anything negative about the people you're selling to, or about your project or about yourself, then the other person has the advantage over you. You have to stay up."

OVERCOMING FEARS

There was a time, says Richard Schwartz about his used book and art store, that the business truly suffered from what he terms his "being too abstracted from the real center of the business, which is there at the street level. Looking back, I realize that by removing myself from the daily dealings with 'Mr. Everyman,' I was succumbing to my own fear of people and my own distaste for and avoidance of the humiliating act of selling something to somebody. These are basic psychological problems that all merchants have to one degree or another."

Schwartz believes that admitting needs and accepting certain limitations has enabled him to get past his fears and to turn the "dialogue with the customer" into the most meaningful and rewarding aspect of the business. The first step, he says, was coming to grips with one inherent problem of dealing in used merchandise, "this thing of not being able to provide what the person wants. There have, after all, been about 50 billion books printed and even if you have 100,000 books, your chances of having what the person wants when he comes in are very slight. And you have to realize that. It's a given in this business.

"It's also a given that it's humiliating to sell something to a person. What you're saying is that you need their money. But you might as well admit that and make something worthwhile out of this particular dialogue.

"The third thing I had to admit was that I really liked people. I like them whether they're very highly developed book collectors or even if they only want to know how much their old family Bible is worth. There's no difference really; we're going to get something out of our relationship no matter what.

"Anyway, all of these fears I think I've fairly well settled in my own mind and that's opened up the business as a way of life. Now when people come in I'm honestly curious about what they want. I want to talk to them about it and if I don't have exactly what they want, maybe I have something similar. I get joy — I mean nothing's greater than to have them walk out three inches off the ground because we've managed to satisfy their curiosity or their need. That's the greatest feeling in the world. That's the opposite side from fear.

"It's a wonderful feeling to recognize that there is nothing beyond the dialogue you have with your clientele that, in itself, is enough to sustain you, to reward you and to make your livelihood. The money — all of that stuff — absolutely has to be secondary. In my own soul I know that the money, the profit motive, is nothing."

So the irony is that if selling represents the most intimidating challenge, it also holds out the greatest possibilities of real satisfaction. Meeting needs, learning, connecting, all come about in the course of the give and take of selling. It only takes a willingness to enter each encounter with a positive attitude.

TAKING RISKS: TO WIN YOU
MUST ENTER THE COMPETITION

"You only have so much control when you're selling. You can do what you feel you can do, and then you're at the mercy of the public."

Joan Robey

For gallery owner Joan Robey, who makes a point of showing work that is "on the leading edge," putting herself on the line simply comes with the territory. Always, her task is to achieve a balance between artistic fulfillment and commercial success, to find work that will represent what she feels is the state of the art and yet will still appeal to her middle-of-the-road clientele. Joan has learned that where public tastes are concerned, no decision is risk-free.

"Sometimes a show will have all the makings of a real success and still be a bomb," Joan observes. "I did a tableware show last year using handmade pieces. Everything was low-priced, pretty and practical. Not only that, I did it in the June wedding season. I thought it would be great for presents. This, I thought, was so safe — I thought it was a guaranteed success. But it was a bust.

"When that happens it forces me to sit down and say, 'Why didn't that work? What do I need to change?' You know, if you're working for someone else, you wake up in the morning, go to work and do your job. Working for myself it's all the time evaluating and re-evaluating and RE-evaluating."

A "TOTAL THRILL"

In the gallery business, says Joan, "there's that feeling every six weeks of being the hostess, that fear of giving an opening and having no one show up, or worse yet, having no one buy anything. The hardest thing is the fear of failure, that I would have gone through all this blood, sweat and tears, put myself on the line financially and personally, made a commitment to it — and then have it flop."

Yes, but when you do go through all that and the show is a smash — now that must be a victory. "No question. When I take that risk and it does pay off it's a thrill — a total thrill!

"The riskiest thing I've ever done turned out to be my most successful show. I had a show last November, featuring a big local artist, and what he was going to be showing was work that was a whole lot more expensive and a whole lot more bizarre than anything he had ever shown to this audience. So those people who had bought his work before, who had paid maybe $300 for a drawing, were now being asked to look at these fancy dolls and collages that were as much as $5,000. Although I thought we would all get a lot of recognition and 'Boy, Joan, that was a really fun opening!' I thought, 'They'll never buy it. They're just too conservative.'

Bill Felder
Freelance Chef

"It started out basically as I had expected. All of his friends came and it was a real fun bash, but nothing sold. It was the first opening I'd done in over a year where nothing sold at the opening, and when two weeks went by without a piece sold, I was starting to panic. I was on the phone calling people, trying to get them in there, trying to make it exciting for people to buy. The artist was getting nervous and I was getting nervous and I was making my employee nervous. Finally I reached the point where I said 'Screw it.' There is nothing more I can do. I have no control over what the people will do. They'll either buy it or they won't. Whatever will be will be.

"It turned around just like that. Within the next month we sold all but four pieces. We got three or four great reviews on the show and it all came together. Totally unlike the tableware show that was such a sure thing and was a bust. This was a totally *unsafe* thing to do, and it's probably been my most successful show."

For Joan Robey — as for many others — the opportunity to achieve this kind of victory is worth the risk of failure. In fact, she says, freedom to take the risks is one of the things she most enjoys about working for herself. "I actually like that fact that when things go bad, there's no boss to blame. I like being responsible for it. And when it goes well, I like to take the glory. And I love to share the praise with the woman who works for me. I like that we're responsible, that no one else makes it happen."

Skillful and consistent marketing is one of the essential elements of any successful venture. From the outset, effective marketing requires not only thoroughness and patience, but also a fair amount of creativity. Often, the greatest challenges will lie in overcoming your own fears. Winning makes it all worthwhile, and ultimately means more than profit.

The Potential of Partnerships

Spend any amount of time talking with men and women in business for themselves and you're bound to hear some strong opinions; perhaps the strongest of all have to do with partnerships. "Never go into business with friends or family!" has become an almost universally accepted, if persistently ignored dictum. There is certainly no shortage of war stories when it comes to partnerships. One woman, when asked to name her greatest business challenge, instantly replied, "The hardest thing was dealing with my partner. As a friend said to me once about going into business with friends: 'Go out and have a drink and kiss the friendship goodbye.' That proved to be true in our case, although now that we're no longer in business together, we get along just fine."

Charlotte Elich-McCall's succinct advice to the beginner is "Do it alone!" Doing it alone is surely one option. One distinct advantage of being your own boss is the prerogative of choosing the people you work with, even if that means working with no one. Still, if partnerships offer the greatest sources of aggravation, they can also be among the most enjoyable aspects of business. Some of the greatest rewards come from sharing the joys and frustrations, the struggles and triumphs, with a partner. Garrett Giann still has some regrets about his partner's moving on. "We worked as a team. We were like brothers." One exhausted and discouraged restaurant owner stated unequivocally that without her "wonderful" partner, she could not have withstood the strain of the first year. "She's the only thing that keeps me going."

Probably the only conclusion to be drawn is that the success or failure of a partnership entirely depends on the individuals involved and the approach that's taken.

WHEN IT WORKS IT WORKS

"I think we were really lucky," says Joan Markowitz, co-owner of MacLaren/Markowitz Gallery. "Business is a lot of hard work and love for what you're doing — and a lot of luck. For instance, our partnership. People are always amazed at how well we work together. In that sense we were really lucky; there are a lot of partnerships that don't work out that well. In our case, the chemistry of the partnership is part of the success of the business."

Looking back on the way the gallery came about, Joan believes the whole venture has been largely an intuitive process. "We started without very much money at all. The business had been in Boulder for years and years as a functional pottery store, a little wooden building on 15th Street that had seen many owners. My mother-in-law saw the business go up for sale and thought she would buy it and set her daughter, who was an art major, up in a gallery business. I had just moved back here and was working there just two days a week. As it happened, the business didn't work out for them, and my mother-in-law sold within a year.

"When she decided to sell I thought, 'Hmm, I've done a lot of things — social work, freelance writing, teaching — but here, at last, I've found the thing I love to do.'"

Joan may have found the thing she loved, but she also knew "there was no way I could do it by myself. I needed a partner." She approached Kathe MacLaren, an artist with the gallery, about going into business together. Kathe had owned a tiny gallery of her own in Taos, New Mexico, and frankly, she says now, taking on another was the last thing she had in mind.

"I thought it was so wonderful to have had the experience because that way I *knew* I would never want to own another gallery."

"It just wasn't the right gallery," counters Joan. "I asked her and within an hour she said, 'Yes, I definitely want to be a partner.' We didn't know where it was going to go —"

"— but we had the same dream for it, to change from ceramics to fine art."

The two women are proud of the way their dream has taken shape. Says Joan, "When we took over it was cups and mugs and couldn't have been doing more than $40,000 a year at that point. We didn't have much money so we had to be very careful, very conservative."

"Sometimes I think we were too conservative," observes Kathe, "but we're still in business and we're doing better every single year."

The partnership might very well be part of the success of the gallery, in that the blending of the two women's tastes has shaped the look and atmosphere of the place. "We're often given compliments on our selection," says Joan. "The gallery is a unique synthesis of our personal tastes; it represents artwork that we like and also feel we have a chance of selling."

Joan Markowitz and Kathe MacLaren
MacLaren/Markowitz Gallery

Kathe continues, "Joan and I have very similar tastes but we also have complementary tastes. We almost always like the same artist but different pieces by that artist, which helps broaden the range of what we offer. Rarely does one of us like an artist that the other one hates, and when we find an artist that we both love, we do incredibly well. It's our enthusiasm for the work that sells it."

Each of the women has collected art for years; it's an important part of their personal lives. "It makes selling so much easier because there's a real truth about it," explains Kathe. "When we discuss a piece with a customer and talk about how art enriches one's life, we believe it. There's no scam." Joan adds, "And we'd be the first to say to a person who's not ready to buy, 'Think about it. If you dream about this piece call me.' We do not promote art as an investment. There's so much misconception about that. Now some of the art we've sold has been what might be considered an investment, because people have bought pieces that have gone up tremendously in price. But that's not the way we promote it. We feel that art is just an enrichment of life. The investment a customer makes is an investment in himself and his environment. It's real easy and comfortable to sell that way."

Joan's eyes glow as she talks about her favorite subject. "We believe in art. We believe in the power of good artwork. When you get a piece of artwork on your wall that's an original — where there's a surface and you can see that it's been touched by an artist's hand — it gives you something every time you pass by it. The greatest reward for us is just seeing the joy art brings to people."

The "Magic" of Limited Partnerships

Often one of the benefits of pooling resources is a greater capital base; more money to invest; a larger cushion to fall back on. Although Kathe's investment was a modest $10,000, it went a long way toward making the changes she and Joan envisioned. Not infrequently, investors are an absolute necessity; partnership is one way of attracting people with money to invest. Emily Hunter, general acting partner in the Briar Rose Inn, tells how a limited partnership made her idea possible.

A single parent with two children, Emily says money was definitely a problem. "I didn't have any real resources of my own, but in the short time I was in real estate I learned about the magic of partnership. As soon as I learned about the concept I realized it was the only way I was ever going to be able to do anything. It's a very simple mechanism: I go to several investors and get, say, $50,000 from each one and put in $50,000 of my own. In a traditional partnership, if I completely botched the whole thing, lost all the money and incurred debts, we'd all be on the line, but this way, the limited partners can only lose what they put into it; they aren't liable for debts incurred. People were more willing to do it on that basis."

How did she find investors? "I was incredibly lucky. I had become very good friends with a woman who was a very experienced investment counselor. She was my contact for almost all of my 12 limited partners. We had no idea how this would go; after all, this was such a novel idea three years ago, at least in this part of the country. I didn't have any sort of track record at all in handling a partnership or running a business, so I sweetened the pot by taking all the liability. But since as the sole general partner I take all the risk, I also get to make the management decisions."

Emily is quite pleased with the way the arrangement has worked out, and recommends that others in her position consider it. "People who are trying to do something without their own capital, if they have energy and an idea, the commitment, then I think a limited partnership offers an opportunity for those people."

Easing Time Demands

Clare Brown, the now retired founder of the first computerized market research firm in the country, has said this about her very successful but highly demanding career: "You must recognize that there's never a turnoff. It's like having a child: Twenty-four hours a day, seven days a week, you're thinking about this business." Sharing the load, says Clare, can ease the strains that tend to dilute the pleasures of owning your own business. "One thing that I rejected all along was to consider a partner, and maybe that was not smart. Now I think if you could find the right, compatible person that you trusted, it would be a good idea. You could go on a vacation and have peace of mind."

Peggy Davenport and Kathie McDonald, of Secret Service Caterers, alternate incoming catering jobs, so that one person isn't exhausted by nonstop demands. "When we get calls," says Peggy, "Kathie and I divide them. She'll handle a party for Tuesday and I'll handle a party for Friday night. That gives us some relief. And you just divorce yourself when it's not your party — we don't check up on each other."

As good a plan as that sounds, sometimes time-sharing doesn't completely solve the problem, if only because neither partner can seem to tear herself away. Joan Markowitz chuckles at the irony. "Someone once said, 'You're so lucky; you have a partner so each of you can work half the time.' I laughed and said 'No, I have a partner and each of us works time and a half.' That's just the reality. There's always something: getting out invitations, getting press releases, contacting clients, finding new artists, reading about art — obviously, if we didn't love it, it would never work."

Complementary Skills

Sheryl and Joe Koch are half of a family-owned stained glass business, a mother/daughter team in which their respective husbands help. Sheryl largely credits their prosperity to Joe's marketing acumen. "I think it's hard for a craftsperson to survive in business because most people who are craft-oriented definitely don't know about business — and you have to have both in order to succeed. I'm very good at making the kaleidoscopes but I'm not very good at collecting old debts and filing receipts, keeping things organized. I did all of it for the first couple of years but I wasn't making any money because I wasn't good at the business end of it. Then Joe took it over and we started making money. We complement each other very well."

Sheryl and Joe Koch, Kaleidoscope Business

In much the same way, Richard Schwartz depends on his partner's business skills to complement his own sales abilities. He gives a graphic example of why both types of skills are needed: "We had a contract with the Salvation Army to buy bulk lots of used books sight unseen. Here we were thinking that we were making ten times our money. We figured we had less than a penny in each book. Then we hired the president of the American Book Seller's Association to do a cost-effectiveness study on our contract. It turned out we were losing money on the deal, that we had 47 cents in each book including our free books and that we were spending way too much money on labor. This is one of the real problems you run into in any business that expands the way this one has. You're so romanced by the profits and not aware enough of the labor intensity it took to get there. We'd be making a lot of money but saying 'Why the hell don't we have more money in the bank?' Well, the answer was we had a lot of cash labor. You unload a truck, you hire guys; you hire other guys to help you sort it. It was in the labor intensity that we were losing all our money. Plus, we didn't realize the honest cost of shelving books. When we did some remodeling, for instance, we needed to temporarily move our books out of the shop and into storage. We spent $9,000 in logistics: taking all the books off the shelves, moving them down the street to storage lockers and then replacing them on the shelves. Nine thousand dollars! Now those are net profit dollars we had to spend.

"That experience taught me that it's going to take me a lifetime to develop any amount of business acumen, to get to the point where I can look at a deal and really psych out the labor, the shelf life, the costs of this thing that go way beyond the basic cost of the product and the sales price. This, I would say, has been the hardest thing for me to learn. That's why I have George, my partner, in there; he's got a more fundamental business sense. I'm more the sales energy and he's more the accountant type."

Complementary Personalities

Kathe and Joan are fond of comparing their different personalities. "Kathe," notes Joan, "has a very strong technical background. Someone once explained to us how it is that we're so effective together by saying that Kathe explains and I emote. Together we cover all the bases."

Kathe admits, "I'm a bit more quick-tempered than Joan," to which Joan hastens to point out, "But we use that to our advantage."

Laughing, Kathe explains, "There are times when it's appropriate to tell someone to get out of the gallery or you're going to call the police. When we want someone who can blow up at an obnoxious customer we send me. When tact is called for we send Joan. There are times you can use strategies like that and it's OK."

"We're very attuned to each other," say Joan. "We can make a sale together. One of us will look at the other and we just know it's time to step in. It's always very comfortable and our customers enjoy watching us interact. By the same token, there might be certain personalities that I might have trouble with or Kathe might have trouble with, so the other one can just step in very naturally so it's not an issue. If you had to deal with those things by yourself it would become much more difficult."

The Value of Moral Support

One partner in a restaurant said the thing she is most grateful for is "not having to face it alone." Peggy and Kathie, of Secret Service Caterers, say that an understanding partner can be a steadying influence when pressures mount. "It's like a marriage," says Kathie. "When one gets more uptight, the other one stays calm. We don't usually lose it at the same time."

The hardest part of business, Kathe MacLaren feels, is keeping your enthusiasm up. "It's hard to always be up for the public. That's why it's so important that there are two of us. Usually either Joan or I can handle it. We were invited to open a second location, but we decided against it and a big reason was that I thought a lot of our success depended on both of us. If you spread yourself too thin over two locations, you know, the highs would be higher and the lows would be lower. This way, we have the partnership to buoy us up and keep us going and keep it fun."

LIVING AND WORKING TOGETHER

Despite all you might have heard about the pitfalls of working with your spouse, there are many advantages to such an arrangement if a couple is able to overcome the obstacles involved.

For one thing, there is a greater likelihood of your spouse understanding the pressures and problems of the work. Unless the husband and wife are both directly involved, it's easy to resent the lack of time together. Chris Finn tells of the problems he had while dating. "I would always explain to any lady I was going out with that once the season started, I'd be swamped. I'd always say, 'It's winter time now; I have all this time. In the summer I have no time whatsoever.' It makes it real hard on a relationship, but if you find somebody who will understand that, it makes it a whole lot easier." Chris married last November; happily, his wife has enthusiastically taken to working right alongside him in the restaurant kitchen.

Common interests can also enrich a marriage, says Brooke Durland, who with her husband Eric, operates "The Adventure Network." "It's been real rewarding working together. We have a lot of similarity of interests and concerns."

Perhaps the best of both worlds exists when one spouse works at another job while the other ramrods the family business, thus creating a blend of companionship and shared commitment to a venture, with the added security of a steady paycheck. For example, Joe Koch holds down a top-level position with Ball Corporation while managing Sheryl's business at home. "We have something in common," he says, "but because I have another job, it's not all-consuming." Sheryl agrees that the arrangement has its advantages. "Because of Joe's salary, we don't have to do it. There's a big difference when you don't have to do something; you can be more creative when you're not under the gun."

POTENTIAL PROBLEMS OF FAMILY PARTNERSHIPS

Of course, the advantage of working with family members also has a flip side. Each plus, it seems carries its corresponding minus and as always, it helps to know about potential problem areas ahead of time. Here are some of the snags to watch out for:

Conflicts Over Who Is Boss

In her book *The Two-Boss Business* Elyse Sommer writes, "Most people we talked with agree that actually working together on one project is the most difficult of all collaborations . . . one partner or the other will probably have to take final charge eventually." The task of establishing authority is further complicated by shifting sex roles. In the Koch partnership, says Sheryl, the lines of authority are very clearly drawn: "Joe's the boss."

Inability to Separate Work From Personal Life

In a recent seminar discussion, a woman offered the opinion that separation of work and personal life is nearly impossible when two people are constantly together. "Twenty-four hours a day togetherness can get to be a real drag," she said. "Have you ever had your husband home on vacation for a week and by the end of that vacation you're saying 'I don't care where you go, just go.'"

Another woman took issue with her, saying that this could be a problem in any partnership. Unconvinced, the first argued, "except that when you're with a partner, at least you go home to your own house and they go home to theirs. You can get a breather, get a fresh outlook in the time you're apart. When I've worked with my husband I've found it very hard to drop the subject of the business."

The Finns tend to agree. Says Brian, "You'll be relaxing on your day off and the first thing that will come up is the restaurant — the 'beast.'

Chris concurs: "If we didn't hold it back to six months, we wouldn't last the whole year. Twelve hours a day is physically draining, but when you add the mental involvement. . . ." Clearly, learning to turn it off represents one of the major challenges facing those in a family partnership.

Blurring of Identities

Two things can happen in a husband/wife partnership, remarks one divorcée who worked with her husband for ten years: "First of all, after a while, you're no longer man and woman but business partners. The romantic, sensitive side of the relationship tends to get stomped to death in the process of making the business go. The other thing that happened in our marriage and business relationship was that when you're both involved in the same work, doing basically the same job, it's hard to tell what the sex roles are and where you fit. I know that in our business, after 10 years I felt I was neither male nor female, but neuter. That came from doing the same thing 24 hours a day together."

Sharing Childcare and Household Duties

Household duties can be a sore spot even in today's presumably liberated climate. A not uncommon scenario is that in which the wife works shoulder-to-shoulder with her husband, putting in the same 10 or 12 hours in the business, but somehow is expected to cook supper when they get home while he flops into a chair to read the paper. Later, long after he will have gone to bed, she'll be up doing laundry. As patently unfair as this is, a surprising number of husbands have real difficulty in changing old habits and assuming their share of the domestic load.

The question of who will tend the children is another potential problem area. One young couple laughed as they remembered coming to the realization that their unexpressed expectations were causing them to bump heads. Toi looked forward to Saturdays when Kevin would be home to take their two little girls off her hands and give her an uninterrupted morning in which to work on her architectural drawings. Kevin had similar aspirations for Saturdays, only in his scenario, Toi would provide the diversions for the kids. After a few Saturdays they saw that some form of compromise was required.

TIPS FOR MAKING A SUCCESS
OF ANY PARTNERSHIP

*"Be careful whom you choose: it's easier to get rid of a spouse
than a business partner."*

Marlene Ospina

While there's nothing you can do to guarantee that a partnership will
work and endure, the following tips will at least shift the odds in your favor.

Start With a Good Foundation

"Around-the-clock harmony is one of those perfect marriage fantasies
many strive for and few attain," writes Elyse Sommer. Probably the best
safeguard against future problems is a foundation of realistic expectations.
"Approaching your business together as a no-lose challenge rather than a do-
or-die mission will help to relieve some fears of failure. Naturally, you hope
to go from A to B, from start-up to success. But if you can really come to
terms with the idea that an end of your business does not spell *personal*
failure, you will release a lot of steam in advance."

Make Expectations Clear

One woman, looking back at an ill-fated partnership, says the basic flaw
was the huge disparity in their motivations for going into business in the
first place. "I needed an income; I had hoped to double my money, whereas
my partner and her husband had viewed the business as a tax write-off. The
difficulties would arise whenever we'd go to buy our inventory together; I
couldn't understand why she was willing to pay so much for things. From the
beginning I didn't realize that she didn't want to make money." The biggest
surprise, perhaps, is that despite the gross misunderstanding, the partnership
lasted two and a half years.

Get it in Writing

Undoubtedly every person who's ever gone into business for himself has
at least one good war story — the one fiasco, the one mistake he wishes he'd
never made. If the business survives, of course, the fiasco becomes a valuable

lesson; the individual emerges much wiser and with some advice for the untried. Charlotte Elich-McCall's advice: "Get it in writing! The times I've gotten into the most trouble and had legal hassles have been in dealing with people and not getting things in writing." Here is Charlotte's war story:

"About three years ago, there was another woman in the area who had a business like mine. She sold a lot of other different craft-related things and we had a pretty good relationship. We'd refer customers to each other. We had this idea that we could have a 'superstore' just by combining our stores under one roof and keeping our identities separate. After trying it for about six months, I felt that it was not the right thing to do. Each of us had separate goals and we had different ways of doing things. Anyway, I decided to end the 'partnership.' She feels I kicked her out and because of all this, we've been involved in a lawsuit for three years.

"You always feel like you can trust people or that each of you knows exactly what's going on when in fact you really don't. Each of you have your own understanding of what's going on and that's what can get you into trouble."

This advice applies for any business relationship, whether it's with friends, family or the shop owner down the street. Setting down an agreement in writing might seem a little formal and a bad omen for husband/wife partnerships, but having a contract, even a handwritten one, can prove very helpful in unsnagging things when an unavoidable dispute crops up.

Defuse Volatile Situations

One way of avoiding conflicts over who will be in charge is to divide the duties of the business. In Brian and Chris Finn's case, delegation of responsibility made all the difference. The two brothers had taken a stab at working together several years earlier when their parents were still active in the operation of the restaurant. Brian, the more volatile of the two, found the "sibling rivalries" more than he could handle and left for two years to attend school in Florida. "We had a hard time working together then because we were both out front working in the dining room." But when the arrangement later changed, Brian reconsidered. "Chris was moving to the kitchen and my parents were getting out of it so I said, 'yeah, that looks like it'll work,' and it does."

Sheryl and Joe Koch maintain a similar understanding, that Sheryl is the artistic expert and Joe has the last word on marketing decisions. Still, flexibility, Sheryl says, is occasionally called for. Take their new model, the Bath Scope, for instance. "When he came out with this last year I laughed at him, but I'm not laughing any longer because they're selling."

One additional tip Joe offers has come about through keeping peace with the California side of the family, Sheryl's mother and stepfather. "We are all human," observes Joe. "You can be an excellent artist or an excellent business person, and then there's *blood*. Competition starts to enter in. I've set some rules. One of the rules is that we don't talk about money. We don't talk about size of business — and that is becoming more difficult as the business gets larger and larger." So while he will say that the business has done very well, he steadfastly declines to name any figures.

Recognize Personal Differences

"We have some highs and we have some lows," admits Sheryl. "I think overall it's turned out real high. We have bumped heads from time to time because we're two totally different people." Sometimes the differences might seem insignificant but in a close working situation, recognizing and respecting those differences can mean getting along. "I can work in a mess and he can't stand it. He has to have everything neat and organized, whereas I can find my way through the clutter to work." Another difference is that Joe is an early riser, preferring to get up about 5:30, puttering around with a cup of coffee in one hand while doing paperwork. Sheryl, on the other hand, is a late sleeper.

Clear up Difficulties Promptly

Brian Finn feels that while friction is virtually unavoidable when working with family members, it doesn't have to become a serious problem. "When you're living close together, you get more involved and can get mad at little things you wouldn't get mad at in somebody else. Even now, we'll get into arguments but we're a tight family so they don't last. They don't mean anything, but when you blow up, you blow up."

"The hardest thing is to stifle it until the night's over," says Chris. "Because you can't do it in front of the employees. That's rule number one. Because the employees tend to take sides and they don't understand that Brian and I can yell at each other and tomorrow it'll be a different thing. They'll come back into work the next day and think that it's still going on."

One entrepreneurial mother feels the same caution applies to children. "They see mom and dad fighting over the family livelihood and become frightened that the family is going to starve."

IS IT WORTH IT?

Despite the risks of conflict — which exist in any partnership — most people say they enjoy working with family and friends. They point to such advantages as similar backgrounds and communication styles, a long track record of getting along. Charlotte has appreciated the freedom to speak her mind to her sister, Donna, who works part-time in the shop. "We really do think alike in a lot of ways. I guess maybe I can say things to her that I sometimes am afraid to say to anybody else." Charlotte admits, however, that occasionally she oversteps herself. "One reason Donna's been working off and on here is that because we're family, I might expect or demand too much of her. After a point she just says, 'Well, this is enough; I'm going to quit.' And she does. I have to say, though, that I've smartened up. I've learned that I really have to watch what I expect of her. If she says she needs some time off, I have to believe her."

"It helps a lot that you've known the people your whole life," says Chris Finn. "You know the right way to go about dealing with them."

Brian agrees, "When Chris and I are having a busy night the communication is rarely verbal, maybe just two words. When he gets behind and I've got people to seat, one of us can read just by facial expressions when the other is in a real bind and we'll adjust to cover the other person. It clicks. That's a real advantage and you couldn't do it with someone you didn't know really well."

"I tried that before Brian came back from school," says Chris, "with different cooks and it always got into a big hassle. Another thing that helps me a lot now that I'm in the kitchen is that I've done Brian's job in the front. That understanding makes it a lot easier."

Perhaps their relationship works because of an essential bond; as Brian describes it, "There's this whole long commitment together. We both have a feeling for the restaurant."

A SPECIAL KIND OF VICTORY

All these glimpses into successful, and not-so-successful working relationships serve to underscore the idea that partnerships are as different as the individuals in them. Because they're comprised of human beings, they can be characterized by any variation of human emotion or behavior. Partnerships can be simultaneously challenging and reassuring, heartwarming and infuriating, and the basis for success and enjoyment probably not available to those who go it alone. There is a special kind of victory when a partnership succeeds.

Kathe MacLaren sums up her feeling about the MacLaren/Markowitz venture with a rare solitary experience. "I remember walking down this street one night and thinking as I walked by our gallery, 'You know, if I didn't already own this business I'd be so jealous of whoever did because it would be just the perfect gallery for me.' And the best part is that we created this. This is, in a way, us."

The Entrepreneurial Family

Given the competing demands of work, school and social life, home life today can take on all the warmth and intimacy of a raceway pitstop, where family members roll in, refuel and roar off again in five different directions. With so little time together, communication is often difficult.

The entrepreneurs in this chapter have found that self-employment can be a way of integrating work, family and personal goals, that work can bring parents and children together in a common enterprise that meets emotional as well as financial needs. How is it possible? By tailoring a business to fit family circumstances.

Self-employment can offer these advantages:

• Built-in time flexibility allows parents to co-ordinate work and other family activities. Parents can schedule days off together and arrange to work while the kids are in school.

• It's possible for parents to work at home at least part of the time in many businesses. Simple physical proximity can help foster feelings of security in children.

• As many families have found, involvement in a common project builds unity and understanding. People who work together with shared goals find communication comes more easily and naturally.

THE ENTREPRENEURIAL MOTHER

The last decade has seen a remarkable increase in the number of female entrepreneurs; according to Department of Labor studies, almost six times as many women as men are starting their own ventures. Furthermore, a significant percentage are married women with children. Here are some reasons for this growing trend.

Owing mainly to inflation, the two-income family has become the norm. More and more frequently today, the second income is used not for luxuries, but for home ownership and the college education most Americans feel is essential.

Although women face a need to earn money, finding jobs in the market place is not always possible or even desirable. For many who don't want a nine-to-five job, starting a business is the only practical answer.

More women are recognizing the value of their own abilities, discovering that skills acquired in the home and community are often readily transferrable to business.

Baby boom women, now reaching their mid-thirties and forties, are taking what they perceive to be their last opportunities to start families. Unwilling to give up hard-won professional status or to turn childrearing over to others, many look to self-employment as a way of combining the two roles.

Ending the Work/Family Tug of War

Janna Haynie frankly acknowledges that profit does not head her list of motivations for tutoring. The most important factors, she says, have to do with coping with the drastic changes in lifestyle that have accompanied the arrival of her three young children, her sudden shift from fulltime teacher to fulltime mother. "The extra income is nice," she says, "but the real value has been the outlet, the contact with other people and with my profession.

"Motherhood plays a very important part in my life," reflects Janna, an earnest, dark-haired mother of three small daughters. "It's a profession for me, a life long chosen. When you think of it as a profession, you have certain goals you want to achieve; you want to give your children everything you can.

Janna Haynie, Tutor

"My husband and I both felt very strongly that the whole inter-relationship of our family depended on our children's getting the best start we could give them. We're both very committed to the fact that children need to have a parent in the home with them in those most formative years before they start their formal schooling."

Taking that stance naturally meant some sacrifices. As committed as she is to fulltime mothering, at least while her daughters are small, Janna admits she missed the mental activity as well as the personal contact of teaching. Those needs, she says, have been to a considerable extent fulfilled by tutoring students in her home. "I think of it as my stimulation, my intellectual outlet. Tutoring is very refreshing and makes me feel like a whole person." Recognizing that her husband's work schedule won't always be so demanding — he is completing his residency as an internist — that he will soon be able to help with babysitting and that the girls will all be in school within a few years, Janna sees a time when she will want to return to teaching. It makes sense to keep her skills in practice. "You use skills and talents rearing children but they're not always the ones you consider to be your professional skills. It's nice to keep those current."

Self-Esteem

One of the things that often suffers when a woman takes up fulltime mothering is her sense of self-esteem, largely because there is little time to tend to her own personal and intellectual development. While it might be a move in the right direction, getting up a half hour early to read or taking an aerobics class is seldom enough. Hobbies are fine, but when you've spent fifteen years developing a skill, a pottery class somehow misses the mark. "Tutoring has been good for my self-esteem," says Janna. "You know little children — they don't say 'Oh, you're such a wonderful mommy.'" She smiles. "I mean there are rewards — there are all those fabulous hugs and kisses, but there's not very much verbal or tangible reward for all the things you do as a mother. You don't get a paycheck.

"I don't regret my choice at all. On the other hand, it's nice to have something that keeps you current in your field and to be working at something you enjoy."

INVOLVING CHILDREN IN THE FAMILY BUSINESS

There is widespread recognition of the need of little children to spend much of their time with one or both parents, but what about older children? While their needs take on a different character, they are no less pressing. When Tom and Judy Haworth bought the Victorian residence that was to become the Vintage Towers Inn, their three daughters were 13, 12 and 10, just the ages when spending money can become an important issue and when children begin to feel a need to know that they're important, contributing members of the family. Tom and Judy saw involving the three girls in the family innkeeping business as a very practical way of building bonds and instilling values. "We wanted to find a business that we could do as a family," explains Tom, "something that would contribute to the girls' understanding of the work ethic and teach them to be productive and supportive of the family as a team. As the girls have grown up they've taken more responsibility. One daughter really likes to wash the clothes and she's good at it; another one's good at mowing lawns and making beds. Last night we were out to a cocktail party. Our oldest was checking in guests."

Now that Ralph Jackson has involved his children in his business, he notices they show a much greater awareness of how the family's income is made. Jackson, an independent consulting engineer, has made a profitable sideline of developing computer software for his clients. From the outset the kids were fascinated by the computer; it was only a matter of time before they asked to be included. Now all three work part-time for his company.

Danny, a 16-year-old high school senior majoring in commercial art, has become proficient enough at computer graphics to be a real help to his father. "He's done a lot of the programming for me. He inputs spread sheets; he did the art work for our business cards and stationery." One project has been a software program for a travel business. "I have to write the manual because I understand all the programs, but Dan's doing all the editing. That's been a very big help to me," says Jackson. "I'm an engineer, not an English major, so I really think he is a stronger grammarian than I am; plus it helps to have someone not as involved as I am sit down and read the manual and get it so it makes sense. He's done a lot of work that we've been able to bill directly to clients."

Ralph, Kimberly, and Cindy Jackson
Computer Business

Daughters Kimberly and Cindy also enjoy working for the company. "They've done typing and editing for me. They know how to run the computer well enough that, for instance with the manual, if I've drafted it and just want to print eight or ten pages, even Cindy, my ten-year-old, will be able to print out the file."

How has working together affected their family relation-ships? "It's been a much more productive and meaningful relationship at what I consider to be the most critical time. The time when you're most likely to lose them is when they start feeling their independence.

"Before, they kind of knew that I worked for the bus company and that was it. Now we'll sit down to dinner and they'll say, 'How'd your meeting go today with so-and-so client?' or 'How's the manual coming?' or 'How are the programs coming?' I think that because they're more directly involved, they have a greater understanding and even respect for me and for what I'm capable of doing. As Dan stands there while I interact with a client, maybe the client's got a complaint or something and we work it out. That increases his respect for me and what I'm able to do.

"The payback of that in the parent role is that when I go to Dan and say, 'Dan, I really think that this ought to be corrected' or 'I really think you ought to go a different direction,' he's likely to think 'Here's that guy who's respected in the community out there. Maybe I ought to listen to what he's saying.'

"I think it also gives you a lot of opportunities to establish credibility with your kids. For instance, if they're trying to do something on the computer I might say to them, 'Now you need to make sure that you do so-and-so or you run the risk of losing a file.' Dan might come back a day later and say 'Dad, that file's completely gone, I can't find it.' 'Well, did you do this?' 'No, I didn't.' Here's a case where he didn't follow the procedures and now he's paying the price for it. Gradually, the kids come to understand that you're not saying things just to harrass them. That builds credibility in a natural way.

"Another thing is that so much of the family relationship is based on simple communication. In our society, we don't have enough things to communicate about with our children. Frankly, a lot of us have been inventing dialogues in order to say that we're communicating with our kids. For me to sit down and talk to Dan or Kimberly or Cindy about something happening in the buisness is a very natural thing now because the business is part of their activity too. Otherwise, for me to sit down with Dan and say, 'Well, how did your day go?' would be contrived. I have no idea what he did and he has no idea what I did, and we're just fabricating a conversation."

A Kid's Perspective

The Jackson children have their own reasons for preferring the new arrangement. For one thing, they are receiving first-hand business experience at an early age. Working in his father's business has helped Danny decide on a career in computer graphics. Since the kids all keep track of their own working hours, entering them on time cards, they are developing a strong sense of the time required to earn a salary. Each is paid with a company check, (rather than going to Dad on Saturday night for an allowance) and they are encouraged to save for the things they want. Cindy's eyes light up as she talks of the hamsters she is saving to buy.

Because Jackson lets them work things out for themselves, learning to use the computer has been a confidence builder. Says Kimberly, "It's surprising what you can figure out. You pick up the manual and at first you don't think you can do it, but if you read it enough times you figure it out and then it's stuck in your head." What if you make a mistake? "When we make a mistake," Cindy says, "we have to go through the instructions and try to figure out what we did wrong. If we can't, Dad will come and help us."

There have been additional lessons. Kimberly says, "In the beginning we used to sit there and procrastinate all the time about how we were supposed to do the work and it would never get done. That doesn't work because everybody ends up getting mad at everybody else, but if you want to work you get excited about it and then it works."

With typical kids' honesty, the two girls happily admit that having Dad around is a definite advantage when they need a ride to a soccer game or a slumber party, or when they have a question. Often, little girls have even less time with busy dads than their brothers. Now that he's at home more, Jackson makes a point of involving himself in their activities, even if it only means setting the table with them.

MEETING CHALLENGES TOGETHER

As exciting as a family venture can be, the rewards, say people who have been there, are not without a price tag. One major investment is that tough, critical building period during which peak effort is required but steady income is not yet forthcoming and freedom and leisure are still dreams. Many families find themselves unprepared for the sacrifices involved, hence marital strife is often named among the top five reasons for business failure. Here, entrepreneurs talk about the two basic challenges facing the family.

Tight Money

According to financial planner Thelton Skipper, one major source of trouble is that spouses are unable to adapt to the insecurity inherent in a fledgling business, the fact that "You're happily rich at some times and dead broke at others. A person might be working hard, putting in a lot of hours but bringing in very little income — enough to pay the rent and eat but not enough to live like they want to. If the spouse can't see what can come out of this, it can cause the person to leave the industry before getting the chance to pay his dues. You've got to have that family support."

Unusual Time Demands

"I could never function having an office at home," says Ralph Jackson. The reason, he explains, is that it's difficult for family members to recognize that even though Dad is at home, he is working. Children especially can resent a parent's being home but nevertheless being unavailable. "At one time," says Jackson, "I was seriously considering moving my office into my home, so over a two-week Christmas vacation I brought all the computer equipment home. It worked well because all the kids were home and they could use it. But there were conflicts of priorities. For example, we had just had the basement remodeled. While we were away in Israel, my brother had reconstructed the room partitions but they weren't finished or painted. At the time, I felt an urgency to be working to generate some income. The family thought it was more important for me to be here painting the walls and getting the room straightened up so they could live here. It finally got to the point where I just said, 'Look, you're going to have to deal with this. I've got to start working.' You constantly have that situation where they don't recognize that you've got to be there at seven or eight o'clock in the morning. You're constantly having to say, 'No, I've got to go to work, I've got to do this.' It's taken a while for them to realize what I was trying to say."

Three Strategies for Dealing With Pressures

As with nearly all problems encountered in business, awareness and preparation can do a lot to reduce strain on the family. Here are some steps you can take:

Financial Preparation

- Lay in a supply of food and commodities

"We have a year's supply of food," says Jackson. "We buy all of our staples on a quarterly basis and we stocked up just before I started this business."

- Build a cash reserve

"Probably the most significant thing I did to prepare financially is that I negotiated three months severance pay when I left my former job," says

Jackson. "That gave me an income to bridge over until my business picked up."

- Lower living expenses

  One very helpful maneuver might be to reduce family debt as much as possible by paying off loans and avoiding any new charge purchases.

- Maintain an alternate income

  A frequently used strategy is for one spouse to remain in a steady job, even if it's only part-time, thereby providing a financial base until the new venture is on its feet.

Creative Solutions

Finding fun, creative solutions to the time/money crunch can actually bring parents and children closer together than if there were plenty of everything, says author Betsy Morscher. During her sixteen years as a single parent, Morscher saw both her career and famly relationships blossom.

After quitting her job, Betsy "mortgaged everything — my house, my car — and went to Europe and began researching preventive health measures. I was gone all summer and when I came back I took five different part-time jobs so I could do my writing. I taught Yoga, belly dancing, Hebrew literature; I wrote resumés, whatever I could find."

Two books and countless magazine articles later, Betsy had established herself in a successful writing and public speaking career. Then, feeling "a real health mission," she began organizing European spa tours to exotic places like Baden Baden and St. Moritz. The aggregate time demands must have been staggering. How did she manage to survive in business without shortchanging her family?

"Usually from Friday night on was my time with the children," she says. "Friday night would be our quiet night where we would just sor of relax and unwind from the week. We would take the phone off the hook and have a special dinner. We lived across the street from a parkwhere there's an elevation; we'd sit and watch the sun setting behind the mountains.

"Because we had very limited resources when my children were small, we learned to develop our talents. I'd encourage them to create songs and dances. I always told them that what Emerson said was correct, that gold and silver were not gifts but only substitutes. The only real gifts were gifts of self. So they would write poems and produce plays for birthdays.

"On Sunday afternoons we would always do something together. We were real pros at finding all the free things. When my children were young the zoo and art museum and botanic gardens were all free. We'd go to band concerts in the park and take hikes around the city. We had all kinds of wonderful adventures."

Adjusting Expectations

The word among weavers is that Charlotte Elich-McCall's store, Skyloom Fibers, has the best stock of knitting and weaving supplies in town. From all parts of the city, craftspeople are drawn to the wood-sided storefront located on a quiet, tree-lined street. Decidedly uncommercial, the store blends in well with the surrounding melange of pre-WWII homes and businesses and present-day novelty shops and natural food resaturants. Inside, Skyloom is large and open and pleasantly crowded with natural yarns of every imaginable color and texture. Downstairs there are baskets from floor to ceiling containing raw materials for weaving baskets; in one corner there rests a spinning wheel. This morning Charlotte is behind the large three-sided counter, moving easily about with her six-month-old baby, Rachel, in a back carrier. Rachel's swing, set up nearby, lends a homey informality to the shop. On the floor, a woman is busy brushing out a blanket; another works over a loom in one corner. The whole scene, underlaid by quiet classical music from the local public radio station, is very serene, almost pastoral. The shop and in fact, Charlotte herself, with her clean-scrubbed face, unstyled naturally curly hair and long dirndl skirt, are both reminiscent of another, simpler era.

Right now, says Charlotte, her biggest challenge is combining the roles of business owner and mother. Despite her surface serenity, she admits that sometimes the demands can be overwhelming. "I don't feel I get a lot accomplished as quickly as I might. I might have a goal of, say, getting the bills paid or something, and find that I didn't even get into the office to do it because Rachel might be having a bad day. Sometimes I just have to put more of my energies toward making her life a little more comfortable and say, 'Who cares if you got an order out?' I have to explain that to customers too, and they've really been understanding."

On the other hand, Charlotte says, smiling, having a baby around the shop has not proved to be completely a disadvantage. Employees seem quite comfortable picking Rachel up and entertaining her if Charlotte is busy with something, plus, a lot of customers have actually said that the baby's generally cheerful presence adds to the homey ambience of the shop. Charlotte grins, "It's kind of neat to come in and not have the shop be so sterile."

Another potential problem, Charlotte notes, is the tendency of the business to become all-consuming, which can be a source of contention if one's spouse and other family members aren't also somewhat involved. "Sometimes you can get really wrapped up — I call it 'hermitize' — in your business. Luckily my husband is sort of in the same position I am. He was in the stained glass industry so he understands working late or having to change all your plans. He and I just don't have a lot of expectations about how much time we have to spend together. We do have Sundays together and I try to arrange my days off to coincide with his days off. He's great too because he's willing to do a lot of the home stuff like making meals and taking care of Rachel as she gets less dependent on me. If I were expected to handle all the domestic chores it would be a lot harder."

Ideally, any decision to go into business should be a family decision, one entered into with commitment and enthusiasm based on an understanding of the sacrifices as well as the rewards. With careful preparation, creative problem-solving and above all, realistic expectations, a family business can be a wonderful livelihood and one of the greatest joint learning experiences imaginable.

Work Issues

A surprising number of new entrepreneurs are unprepared for the drastically increased time and energy demands self-employment brings. As your own boss, they learn, you may technically have the freedom to work your own hours; in reality (in the beginning, at least) you typically trade nine-to-five for nine-to-nine. One man was attracted to construction work because the steady, predictable schedule would mean having evenings and weekends free to spend with his family. The reality was somewhat different, however: "the fact is if you're working for yourself, you may be home at night but you're doing the paperwork, and if something goes wrong you do work on weekends."

A freelance writer and lecturer says, "I think it takes a rare breed of person to go into business for himself because you're not talking a 40-hour week; you're talking an 80- to 100-hour week. You're talking commitment, discipline, enthusiasm when there is none. I think that talent and creativity are wonderful, but I really think the key ingredient in business is perseverance."

"Make sure you really want to do it," is Warren Paul's advice. "Make sure that you really want to put in the time. Eighty hours is nothing. Putting in 80 hours a week is like putting in the ante in a poker game. It doesn't mean you're going to win — it just gives you the right to play the game."

In this chapter, we'll examine the logistics of putting in the sometimes staggering hours, the reasons people are willing to do it, and some ways to make it all worthwhile. We'll see how entrepreneurs get into the game *and* win.

THE COSMIC JOKE

Richard Schwartz, whose Stage House II Books sells used books and prints, admits that the reality of the business has not measured up to his pre- startup dreams. "I thought if I had this used bookstore I could sit and read all the time and write, both of which I love doing, and I would converse with intelligent people and have a very nice dialogue and solve all the problems of life. It would be a wonderful existence and I'd probably make a lot of money too. The cosmic joke on me is that since I got into this business, I have not had time to read or to write. There's always way too much to do when you're in business for yourself."

Schwartz isn't alone in his assessment of the way things are. Donna Hudgel, who for years had harbored a love for all facets of Western Americana, thought that opening her own bookstore would be the perfect way of satisfying her thirst for knowledge. Like Schwartz, she found that running her own store left little free time during business hours. "There is no time for reading. It's before or after working hours like everyone else."

Hudgel's store seemed pretty quiet on this afternoon; what does she spend her time doing? "Paperwork. One observation I've made, ever since I first had the idea of having my own store, is there is always a cluttered desk in every bookstore. If the front desk was clean there was a desk tucked back in some little room that was just dreadful with paper. I hoped it wasn't true but it really is; there is a lot of paperwork involved."

THE GLAMOUR MYTH

When entrepreneurs are disappointed by the realities of their businesses, often it's because they were drawn to a career not by a love for the work itself, but by the supposed glamour surrounding it. The best analogy is probably the aspiring starlet who migrates to Hollywood to fulfill a dream. It's the trappings of stardom — the parties, the openings, signing autographs, hobnobbing with other stars — rather than an abiding love for the craft of acting that drives her. When this is the case, disappointment usually follows because, sadly, the glamour of any business is generally only a very small part of what it's all about.

"Art Schleppers, Inc."

"Joan and I often laugh," says Kathe MacLaren, "because there are a lot of people who come in and want to work for us and think it's so wonderful. It's as if every doctor's wife goes into the gallery business because it's so 'glamorous' and so 'easy' and 'fun' to 'sell pictures.'"

"What's glamorous about it is being constantly surrounded by something that's important to us and something we feel is important beyond itself," explains Joan. "It's not like selling shoes. Shoes can be very beautiful but after the initial rush of going to New York and buying the new fall line, there isn't that thrill when you open a box of shoes that we have when we open a box of who-knows-what from artists all over the country. Truthfully, it is wonderful working around the artwork, but as you can see there's an awful lot of schlepping and cleaning and calling — just regular old hard work. About 80 percent hard work."

If You Just Want to Be a Star, Forget It

"I think some people who start magazines are frustrated artists or photographers or writers, and some people start them because they want to be popular in the community or in the world. My purpose for starting was to make a good business out of something that I loved to work with: words and pictures." Garrett Giann is explaining his reasons for leaving a lucrative career in real estate in order to publish *Colorado Homes and Lifestyles*. While the magazine's circulation might be considered modest — around 25,000 — it's a classy publication for people who are interested in home design, gardening, entertaining, travel and the arts. "Ultimately the magazine is intended to give people a good feeling, maybe even have an elevating effect. It's something people can look at and say, 'Hmmm. That's nice.'"

Giann says that publishing a magazine was initially intended to be a creative outlet. "In real estate I could make a lot of money by just moving deeds around, but it didn't build the buildings; for me, being a real estate broker was pretty uncreative." The magazine, he hoped, would fulfill that need.

"It did when I started," he says, "but not now." What changed?

"I think the demands of the business overwhelm the creative part. The magazine is creative but like any business it doesn't succeed because it's creatively excellent; it succeeds because it's run as a business. Unfortunately, the creative part comes much easier for me than the details of the business. It's more difficult to hire the right receptionist than it is to select the right picture for the cover."

Tight Budgets: The Mother of Ingenuity

Although tight capital is often the prime difficulty in launching a new business, particularly something like a magazine, Giann says money has not been the biggest challenge. Besides, he points out, "corporate magazine startups aren't guaranteed successes just because they have unlimited capital. The most spectacular successes in magazine history were started by people who had very little money. The *Reader's Digest,* was started in a garage. They were very thinly capitalized and they made a go of it."

Was *Colorado Homes and Lifestyles* a similar success story? "Yes and no. We started with very little; I had more than $5,000 but nothing close to the $2 or $3 million you're supposed to have to start this kind of magazine. It forces you to do certain things, though: to live cheaply, to spend $7 on something instead of $25.

"Somehow one of the laws of the universe is that if you have it you'll spend it, and that goes for time too. If you have a lot of time you'll use it. Magazines sometimes have too much time to think. You can sit all month long and say, 'Well, what do we want to do next time?' You can burn up a lot of money that way. Ingenuity is forced upon you when you don't have much money and that's good."

If money hasn't been a primary difficulty, what has made the business such an enemy to creativity? Certainly the sense of achievement that comes with seeing each finished issue come off the presses must keep the creative juices flowing from month to month.

"I think from time to time you get a sense that you've achieved something that was a lot more difficult than you ever imagined, so you take satisfaction in that. But I'll be honest; the fact that it takes minute after minute, day after day to get to the achievement dulls the reward. You'd think that you'd feel a lot of satisfaction because it took so much work, but it's just the opposite; it kind of dulls the satisfaction." He chuckles. "It's like the hostess who works hard all week planning and preparing a dinner. There's this nice little dinner party, they light the candles and then eight people gobble up the food in ten minutes."

One aspect of magazine publishing that makes it difficult to sit back and enjoy the finished product, says Giann, is the fact that there never really is a finished product. "There's never an absolute moment when it's complete," he explains. "Even as you're getting an issue off the press, you're worrying about the other issues you're planning to produce. Unless I sell the magazine, it's never over."

To be fair, not everyone would find the ongoing demands so oppressive. Giann allows that some publishers may thrive on the very pressures he describes. The object, he says, is not to be drawn into a business by the illusion of glamour. "Make sure that you want to do it as a business and not because you want to be somebody at the country club. Don't start a magazine just because you love magazines. You have to love the business part of it or you won't make it.

"I think it's the same in everything, whether you're a basketball player or a doctor or whatever: Your natural abilities are what got you into it and your love of it may have kept you in it, but the thing that makes you great is your discipline and your tenacity and your perseverance — and your willingness to take the good with the bad. If you just want to be a star, forget it."

MAKING IT WORK

Frequently the difference between enjoyment and drudgery is a person's attitude toward the task. Maybe the reason so many entrepreneurs are willing and happy to work incredibly long and hard hours is the fact that they chose the work for themselves. It's very different when you're working for yourself, they say. You basically like what you do on a daily basis.

"You work a lot harder when it's for yourself," observes Warren Paul, "but I love it. I would never work this hard for someone else. I mean there are weeks that I put in 100 hours — not every week, but when I first started this store I was putting in 120 hours a week for about two months because I was building this place. I would never do that for someone else. It wasn't easy but I was willing to do it for myself."

Was it because of the knowledge that he was building something for the future? "If I really think about it, part of it is the idea of building something, but on a day-to-day basis, it's just the sheer enjoyment of doing it. If you really enjoy what you're doing it doesn't matter."

Work Can Be Energizing

"Everybody thinks I'm so blitzy, that I move too quickly and that I'm too like a New Yorker," remarks Richard Schwartz. "It's really the enjoyment. The reason I move fast is because I'm having fun.

"It's also because there's always way too much to do. When you're in a business that you've made yourself and you're basically a disorganized person — and most used book and art dealers are tremendously disorganized; when

when you see them in their store, even if it looks impeccable it's just a front. That's why they never let you in their bathrooms or their basements!" He laughs heartily, enormously amused at this apparently universal failing. "But anyway, the reason I move so fast all the time is I'm getting enjoyment out of what I'm doing and that, I'm convinced, works itself into a physical energy. Just the enjoyment itself drives my adrenals."

"It's Mine, That Makes Me Care"

For the first four years after opening her retail yarn business, Charlotte Elich-McCall operated the shop virtually single-handedly. Until four years ago, when she felt she could afford to hire an employee, she was alone in the store most of the time. Often, she remembers, her days would begin at eight in the morning and end at midnight. Long after closing she would stay on, putting away shipments and doing paperwork. Today, while she no longer has to do everything herself, she still spends many hours working in the store. It says something about her love for the business that she doesn't feel particularly burdened.

"I like having responsibility and making decisions, solving problems," reflects Charlotte. "I think you have a lot of freedom when you have your own business. One thing I didn't like about working for Ray was that after a while, every month seemed the same. At the beginning of the month you had all the reports, and on the fifteenth of the month you had this to do and at the end of the month you had to get all of this organized to close the month. Month after month just felt like it was all the same. Here, I still have things I have to do at certain times during the month, but it seems real different. Maybe it's because I like the media, yarn and people working with their hands. It seems to me a whole lot more interesting than what I was doing." What about working at the fabric store? Wasn't that working with textiles and dealing with people who worked with their hands? "Yes," admits Charlotte, "I was kind of working with the same people but I didn't have the same feel for it. I didn't really care then if they bought blah-blah-blah fabric or whatever. Here I do. Because it's mine, that makes me care."

Antique dealer Pauli Wanderer has a firm handle on her attitude toward the task: "When I get down on the business, it's because I've forgotten that my main motivation is to wake up in the morning and like what I do. Generally I wake up in the morning and say, 'Boy, I'm sure glad I do this rather than going to some damned office.' There's enormous satisfaction in that."

Immersion: When You'd Rather Work Than Do Anything Else

"The nature of my work keeps me happy," says cartoonist Meg Biddle. Does she worry about the creative well running dry? "I know it's not going to run dry — there's no possible way. If nothing's coming from here," she taps her temple, "you just have a conversation with somebody and it pops up. I'm a very social person. Interaction is where I get my ideas.

"It truly takes a thief. You take situations and record them. When you go to sleep at night and you think of something and you want to write it down, you do it, whether that night or the next morning. You just have to grab them when they're happening and record them.

"You've got to be prolific. You've just got to keep working. You can't work just for a client, you have to work for yourself. Once when I was feeling kind of low and depressed I drew all day long and as a result I got a fresh portfolio. You've just got to keep doing it." In fact, one of the things that makes Meg's work so effective is the way she is able to capture the humorous slant on mundane occurrences everyone can relate to.

Overcoming Creative Blocks

"In terms of individual cartoons, get rid of the idea that each one's got to be a masterpiece. Boy, that's a tough one!" she sighs. "If I'm away from cartooning for a week and a half, I start thinking, 'Boy! This one's going to have to be *excellent!*' You start thinking you've got to make up for all this lost time and you become frozen.

"But I'm learning to overcome that. For instance, this last month I took some time to visit my sister in Philadelphia, who had just given birth to a baby boy. I mean this kid had the biggest nose. I just went nuts and drew him every night before I went to sleep. As a result they have a million cartoons of their newborn that they love and I kept drawing. That's why I say you've got to be prolific. Not everything will be publishable, but you've got to keep doing it for exercise. It's like letting your body go: You can be away from it for just a short time and start feeling it."

The Beauty of Enthusiasm

For people like Kathe MacLaren and Joan Markowitz, immersion in their work is not so much a necessity as it is enjoyment. Part of the fun, they agree, is talking about art — their mutual passion — together. "We can't get enough of it," exclaims Kathe. "When we go to New York, it's one gallery after another, talking all the time!" Joan adds, "We read a lot about art, not just the things that we carry, but all kinds of art, and we're always discussing the things we read. One day we were out driving around in the Volvo, blabbing away about the nature and merits of contemporary sculpture, not really watching where we were going because we were so involved in the conversation. Anyway, I made this turn onto Broadway. I looked up and suddenly realized there were four lanes of traffic converging on us. I had driven a whole block going the wrong direction on this one-way street."

The Importance of New Ideas

Peggy Davenport, of Secret Service Caterers, feels that an important part of her job is keeping abreast of changing tastes and new trends. That means constant perusal of cookbooks and culinary magazines, combing them for ideas. Using a variety of menus is important, she says, especially if you're doing several parties each year for the same client. "When you have one group of people that you're working with — we've done a lot of parties for the art museum — it inspires you to come up with new and different ideas. It keeps us more interested too, because after you've made 5,000 pieces of sesame chicken it's fun to do chicken paprikabobs for a change." Looking for and trying out new recipes can be one of the most exciting aspects of the business, says Peggy. "It's fun! Instead of getting into bed with *War and Peace,* I get into bed with *Bon Appetit.*"

MAXIMIZING PRODUCTIVITY AND ENJOYMENT

Let's face it, there is sure to be a heavy time/energy drain, especially at first. The trick is to make the hours count. That means learning how and where to spend your time in order to reap the greatest possible return for your investment.

"Smart Hours"

"Naturally, the more hours you put in, the quicker the payoffs come, but you have to learn to put in 'smart hours,'" says Thelton Skipper. Smart hours, explains Skip, are income-generating hours. "I mean we can sit here and shuffle papers all day long, but that's not productive time. If I don't have a client in front of me I'm not employed.

"Now that paper shuffle is necessary. You've got to have those hours where you're on the telephone calling people, but you have to understand that those tasks don't actually generate income. They're not billable hours. What I often do is come down here at two o'clock in the morning when I can't be out with a client and use that time to shuffle paper."

Time Management

"Time takes on a whole new dimension when you're on your own," says Ralph Jackson. "I'm much more conscious of productively using time. If I'm going to bill a client for an hour I want to make sure he's got an hour's worth of work out of me. In a bureaucracy you don't tend to worry a whole lot about that. You're gonna get that paycheck anyway. If you take 15 minutes to talk to somebody about a family problem or whatever, you're still going to get the same paycheck. But in my business, I'm not going to bill a client for 15 minutes of talking to somebody about something that doesn't relate to that client. So time takes on a totally different dimension.

"You have to work much harder at managing your time. With your own business there are a lot of little things that you can get caught up in 'til you're spending all your time there and not getting the client's work done. You can make trips to get office supplies or get more discs or go out to look at hardware or software or spend time talking about different ways to do the accounting system — just a myriad of those kinds of things that tend to look like they're important and need to be done.

"I've used fairly organized time management procedures for years, setting objectives at the beginning of the week for what I wanted to accomplish, breaking that down into tasks, deciding when I'm going to do those tasks during the week. What I've had to do since starting this business is intensify that effort: figure out what I want to accomplish this week and when I'm going to do it, who I have to contact, exactly what kinds of things I have to do. I find that if I do that, things pretty well get done. If I don't take the time to do the planning, I go through two or three days and not a whole lot gets done."

Establishing a Work Structure

It is universally acknowledged among people who have cut themselves loose from nine-to-five schedules that without discipline and some kind of structure, freedom to work one's own hours can be as much a problem as an advantage. Properly managed, however, freedom to decide how to spend your time can be one of the most enjoyable aspects of being on your own. Recalls Jackson, "One of my frustrations at the transportation agency was that they were an eight-to-five organization. They expected you to be there from eight to five regardless of what the circumstances were. I remember the night that I worked there until five in the morning to get something done and then at eight-thirty the next morning I was chastized because I was a half hour late for work. That kind of thing. . . . Last night I was on the phone to Israel until one o'clock in the morning doing what I had to do there. Well, since I'm in charge I can say, 'Okay, this morning I'll take care of some other things and it'll all balance out.' There's the freedom to say 'I'm going to do what I know is right and I'm going to do it when I need to do it.' If the family has a need or one of the kids has something at school and I want to take an hour in the middle of the day to go do that, I can do it and work in the evening if I want to."

Delegation vs. Doing It All

Often the very hardest thing to do is to delegate responsibility to others. For one thing, it's hard to relinquish control and perhaps for good reason: it may be that no one you can hire can do the job as well as you. Another difficulty may be the feeling that unless you're doing it all, you're somehow falling short; for some, self-esteem is tied up in total self-reliance. For example, after years of struggle, one professional singer arrived at a level of success where demands upon her time were greatly multiplied. Faced with hiring an agent, a business manager and a musical director, she balked: "If other people handle all those things, won't that make me worth less?" "No," replied her patient personal manager, "that will make you the boss." Ask yourself this question: "Is this the most important thing I could be doing right now? Should I really be addressing these mailers or should I let a secretary do it?"

One chore few entrepreneurs like is keeping track of the business books. Ralph Jackson has decided that particular task is something he can well afford to turn over to someone else. "Managing all the accounting and getting that separate from the family finances is, to me, somewhat of a frustration because I find I have to spend a lot more time at that than I would like to. That whole aspect of management has been more of a chore than anything else. It's not particularly hard, just tedious and bothersome.

"I decided not to go to an accountant but to sign a contract with a firm that specialized in handling the books for businesses that are too small to have their own accounting departments. The company I'm using charges $75 a month, which in my view is not a whole lot. In fact, when I started out using a regular accountant, paying him by the hour, I went double that the first month."

The difference, explains Jackson, lies in the way the company has systemized the job. "You're supplied with a special checkbook that makes a double entry. You give the check to one person, send the copy to the accounting service. All they do is feed the information into their computer and the computer does all the work. They have it fully automated and because they have so many small businesses as clients they use great big computers that are very efficient. So you essentially have the accounting capability of a huge firm.

"The alternative I've explored is to go buy an accounting software program for about $600 and do it myself. I'd have to learn how to use the software, which wouldn't be that difficult, but I'd lose out on the company's expertise. The guy who handles my account knows all the tax laws; he advises me on what to do to give myself the greatest tax advantage. If I were running my own software I wouldn't get any of that, simply because there's no way I'm going to spend a week every year learning all the new tax laws.

"The net result is that they're probably saving me 10 to 12 hours a month. I bill my time at $50 per hour, so that's between $500 and $600 a month that they're saving me, not counting the tax savings they are able to achieve through their expertise."

AVOIDING BURNOUT

What is burnout? In the simplest terms, it is a condition of physical and emotional bankruptcy produced by working too hard, too long in a high-pressure environment, observes psychologist Bonita L. Perry. Ironically, Perry believes, failing to control the duration and intensity of work can be worse than not working hard enough. Why is burnout a particular problem for entrepreneurs?

• When you truly love what you do, it's simply hard to call it a day.

• Financial insecurity is frequently a strong motivator. When you work for yourself, a paycheck is not a twice-a-month given; income can no longer be taken for granted.

• Often, self-employed people work at home. Shutting off is harder simply because you can't get away from the work environment. The undone paperwork is there staring you in the face.

• The drive to achieve is powerful in most entrepreneurs. "I had a very strong father who was an important role model for me," reflects Patrish Wiggens. "He had nine children so he was always there hustling, trying to provide. He had sales ability. I was number five, right in the middle, so I've always been a struggler. With four older, I was always struggling to live up to their achievements. With four younger, I always had to babysit.

"We didn't have the traditional male/female roles in our home. Everybody did everything. My mother, with nine children, always stayed at home and she never seemed happy. That had a profound effect on me. I said, 'I'm not going to have nine children. I'm not going to stay at home all the time.' So from the beginning there was this strong push to hustle, to distinguish myself."

Attitude Adjustment

Acquiring a healthy attitude toward work is the first step in burnout-proofing yourself. It's helpful to get rid of certain misconceptions about work and its relationship to success. One major misconception is that non-stop, frenetic activity results in the greatest productivity. Dr. Layne Longfellow, Ph.D., a psychologist who specializes in education for top-level executives describes the attitudes he frequently encounters.

"Talk to Type A's (the quintessential workaholic) and they will say that 'only my Type A behavior got me where I am and it's the only thing keeping me here.'" The truth is, says Longfellow, that these people succeed not because of their Type A behavior, but in spite of it. He cites one 40-year study of Harvard graduates which showed that the most successful men were not the workaholics but those who were able to achieve a balance of work, family and social life, to relax and have fun.

The Great — and Small — Escapes

For Tom and Judy Haworth, who not only run The Vintage Tower Inn but also live on the premises, being on call 24 hours a day can be taxing, to say the least. It's helped, says Tom, to "take the phone off the hook at night to keep people from calling at three in the morning to make a reservation." An easy-going personality also helps. "I genuinely like people and can tolerate a lot of interruptions at odd times," says Tom. "I'm from a big family — seven kids — so I'm used to it."

The greatest safety valve for the Haworths, however, has been the practice of periodically getting physically away from the business — and each other — for a time. "Sometimes separate vacations are a good idea," remarks Tom. "I went sailing in the Bahamas on my own for a couple of weeks a couple of years ago. This month my wife is going back east to visit her relatives. Our daughters take off and sleep at girlfriends' houses. At least once a week someone's gone somewhere." While separate vacations are nice, Tom feels the best escapes are those the whole family earns and enjoys together. "Every year the business has grown nicely. Last summer it had grown enough that we hired people to take over for a month while we all went off to Europe."

Some types of self-employment can be the best of all possible worlds for those who like to travel — by making it possible to both get away and write off the expense. This is one aspect of business that came as a pleasant surprise to Charlotte Elich-McCall. "I didn't know when I started how big a part travel can play in what I'm doing. I went to New Zealand for a month about two years ago and the whole trip was geared around finding things for the store. I realized that what we do here is done everywhere; in every country you're going to find weavers or creative people working with their hands, either in manufacturing or cottage industries. I can take a trip anywhere and it can revolve around what I'm doing. Someday what Chris and I want to do is buy a sail boat and sail away." Is that a possibility? "Definitely," replies Charlotte. "I think that what I'm building here is going to make that a reality one day. I'm the sort of person that says, 'If you're gonna do it, just do it.'"

Mental Health Time

Author Betsy Morscher, who used writing as a springboard for her own travel business, says "One of the things that really kills people, especially in the service industries, is that often we give and give and become so altruistic that we've nothing left for ourselves. I really believe what the Jewish sage Hillel said was true: 'If I'm not for myself, who am I? If not now, when?' I think I have to give to myself first and then I can give to somebody else. So I always carve out a little oasis in the middle of the day to meditate. Or I take a walk or I listen to classical music.

"My kids are real funny because they know there is certain music that will help me when I'm really tired or stressed. I remember that right after I was married (to second husband Gordon Edolls), I had stayed up for two nights in a row writing. Gordon said to the kids, 'Your mother seems so tired and can't seem to relax.' My teenage son clued him in. 'Well, if you'll just let her go to bed with Mozart, she'll be fine.'"

Creating Mental Separation

If physically getting away is impossible, there are still ways of mentally closing the door on work. Brooke Durland says that in addition to taking frequent weekend trips, she and her husband also take turns running interference for each other at home. "We make it a point to say, 'This is *your* time. Do what you want.' Then we really focus on the idea of 'This is my time; I'm going to choose how I want to spend it.' Like Sunday afternoon, Eric took the kids and — well, I took a nap. It was my choice. No guilt attached."

One home-based businesswoman has created a ritual for herself to mentally close up shop. At five o'clock, she says, "I go out the front door, close it, stand there on the step a moment, then turn around and come back in. As I come through that door, it's with the idea that I'm finished for the day."

The Perfectionism Trap

"When everything has to be right, something isn't."

Stanislaw Lee

According to Bonita Perry, the major culprit in burnout is what she calls the perfectionism trap. Perfectionism, she asserts, "is not the healthy pursuit of excellence by men and women who take genuine pleasure in life, marked by true accomplishments. Perfectionism is setting standards which are unnaturally high beyond reach or reason. It is straining compulsively and unremittingly toward impossible goals. It is measuring self-worth entirely in terms of productivity and accomplishment."

The perfectionist expects too much of himself and others. Because he sees himself as forever and irredeemably inadequate, he fails to take satisfaction in the things he does accomplish. Inevitably dissatisfaction turns to fatigue, ennui, emotional burnout. The antidote is simple enough to understand if often hard to practice: Lighten up on expectations of flawlessness.

Accepting limitations and human failings has decidedly helped grease the wheels of the MacLaren/Markowitz partnership, and is one of the reasons the relationship is still going strong after five years. Says Joan Markowitz, "We each have our shortcomings. If Kathe screws up, she'll be incredibly apologetic and I'll say 'Look, if you hadn't done it, I easily could have done it and probably will.' We realize that we're both human."

The Importance of Humor

You must have a sense of humor," says Joan. "There are a lot of things that happen in business that you have to kind of look at in a philosophical, humorous way. You have to know what to take seriously and what to let go. A sense of humor gets you through."

As a case in point, Kathe remembers the time she decided to put an ad in the paper with both of their pictures. Her reasoning was clear enough: "I thought it was important to have personal identification. We both thought people would feel more comfortable knowing who they're buying from. Well, naturally, the only person who called from that ad turned out to be this guy who made porno movies — he was looking for new talent!

"We have some fabulous stories," she laughs. "Joan and I have decided that we're not going to get rich off the gallery — we're going to get rich on the book we're going to write about all our escapades."

It *Can* Get Worse

It would be hard to find a person who has been in business for any length of time who hasn't weathered at least one near disaster that, in hindsight, proved to be funny. Brian Finn recalls one night at the Gold Hill Inn with particular "warmth."

"Don't ever say, 'Well, at least it can't get any worse,'" warns Brian, laughing. "One night — it was a Friday and we were really busy — we'd just hit our peak when the electricity went out. We were just going crazy. We had all these people, Chris had all these orders on the line. So we went through all this ruckus getting everything together and finally got through the night. After it was over we were all saying, 'Whew! At least it couldn't get any worse!'

"The next night, Saturday night, it was even busier. Chris had been holding me off, not letting me seat any more people; he had tickets all over. I was just about to walk back to the kitchen to plead with him to let me seat this one group of people because they were getting uptight." But when Brian walked through the kitchen door he couldn't believe his eyes. They had just acquired a new oven which, it turned out, had been installed too close to the heat sensor of the fire extingusher. "I walked in and the whole place was covered with CO_2. Chris had 15, 20 steaks on the grill, all the sauces, so all those orders that were up were wiped out. Everybody was stunned. I started hyperventilating.

"And then that whole kitchen just came together. Everybody from the dishwasher to the salad maker was just going whoosh! Chris just started throwing things in the sink, got a broom and swept off the line and started back up again, made new sauces and we were serving dinner 45 minutes later.

"I went around to every single group that was waiting out there and I told everybody to go around to all the people in the dining room. I said, 'You explain to them exactly what happened.' And not one person got upset. And we did it. We got it together."

One of life's little excitements.

No one would argue that being your own boss is easy or relaxing; whether you're taking over a business or starting one from scratch, it's going to mean long, intense hours of work with minimal returns at first. But if you go at it right — and put into practice some of the tips offered by the people in this chapter — you can make it work in the long run.

The Artisans

Working at an art or craft — and making a living at it — can be the happiest of lifestyles. It might be color on canvas, the earthen elements of clay, the beautiful precision of language, or the ecstasy of disciplined movement through space; there is undeniable satisfaction in doing the work, regardless of who else sees it or how much money is made from it. Devotion to a craft both defies explanation and makes justification unnecessary.

Then too, the skill, patience and refinement that come with pursuing artistic perfection can affect an artist's character in ways that spill over into every aspect of his life. Communication, for example, takes on a new dimension. Through art, it is possible to touch others in ways that are otherwise inconceivable.

Many would agree that if you could somehow manage to get yourself into a career that pays these kinds of dividends, it would be nothing short of a dream come true. The good news is that it's possible. The people in this chapter have done it and so can you. On the other hand, the words "starving artist" wouldn't have become the cliche they are if it were easy. Although it is an achievable fantasy, it's rarely easy and here are some reasons why:

THE IMPORTANCE OF COMMERCIAL APPEAL

As soon as you decide to become a professional, your artistic discretion is no longer unlimited. It's as if you'd taken on your buyers as partners; instead of painting for yourself, you must now consider other people's tastes and compromise — anathema to many artisans — becomes part of the equation.

THE NEED FOR BUSINESS ACUMEN

Traditionally artists have considered money a sullying influence, or have felt they just didn't have the time or the head for tasks like bookkeeping. But even with an agent or business manager, it's hard to succeed and remain wholly insulated from the business side of your livelihood.

TIME IS MONEY

"My priority is making something I'm proud to be associated with," says stained glass worker Sheryl Koch. As a matter of fact, the quest for excellence is the driving force behind virtually all artisans. The problem is that excellence takes time. Relatively few artisans are able to really charge enough for a finished work to justify the hours invested.

One woman who makes lovely shawls for family members must constantly turn down requests from admirers. "The cost of my time alone," she explains, "would make the price astronomical." Looking back on his beginnings, potter John Hansen says "I wouldn't even want to think of what I made per hour the first few years. It was a labor of love."

FLUCTUATING DEMAND

"During the Christmas season it was so crazy," remembers Sheryl Koch. "You've got to get all these orders out — I could work till midnight every night and still there would be so much to do." Keeping up with periods of peak demand is the continual bane of the ultra-small business. The question for the sole operator seems always to be, "Should I try to gear up or just pass up the business? Should I hire another person? Build up my inventory? Should I invest in more equipment that would handle peak demands but probably sit idle the rest of the time? These are headaches for any small business but especially for the person whose business depends on superb quality. If one-of-a-kind originality is part of the appeal, gearing up may not be an option.

COMPETITION, A FICKLE PUBLIC

People commonly reason that careers in the arts are precarious because in a depressed economy non-essentials are the first to go. To a certain extent, that's true. On the other hand, when times are hard people need the escape provided by art, and seek to have beautiful, uplifting things around them. More often the threat to security comes not from the economy but from changing tastes and interests. No matter how popular an item is, the odds are good that eventually its market will wane. "It's not going to last forever," says Joe Koch of the phenomenal success of Sheryl's hand-crafted kaleidoscopes. "We're one of the top sellers in the country but it's not going to go on indefinitely." Another factor is competition. Sheryl predicts that "one of these days somebody from Taiwan is going to come over and figure out a way to make these much cheaper. It's just inevitable."

Enough cautions. All these points are not meant so much to discourage you as to arm you; once prepared you can devise ways of getting around the snags.

HOW SOME PEOPLE BEAT THE ODDS

"Mini Mass-Production": John Hansen, Potter

"I think it's a big dream of people to take something they like doing and make it into a business," says John Hansen. "But I don't think most people are prepared for the sacrifices and the tainting of what they love doing when they do it as a business. You have to be able to compromise." Hansen made a conscious concession in order to enjoy the rewards of his art and the advantages of self-employment; his compromise, mass production, has netted him the things that matter most to him.

Hansen never seriously considered pottery as a career. Although he had long enjoyed the craft, he'd decided the starving artist route was not for him. Instead he spent his post-college years teaching, working in TV, finally managing an employment agency. Then came the near catastrophe that changed his life. While not exactly compelled by circumstances, he did make the most of what could have been considered a disaster, using it as a springboard to a whole new career.

John Hansen
Potter

What happened is that Hansen broke his leg in a skiing accident and because of improper medical treatment the leg didn't heal. With complications and several remedial surgeries, his recovery stretched out to well over two years.

"I spent the whole two and a half years recuperating from the complications of the accident right here in my studio. I was about $14,000 in debt because the last two operations weren't covered by insurance." Pottery, he says, became a sort of vocational therapy. "It kind of kept me off the street. I had those bills to pay, plus I liked it. It was something I was good at and the time went quickly. If it weren't for this, I wouldn't have survived the frustration of those two years."

The studio, originally a chicken coop, is conveniently located right in John's backyard. A few years ago he built on the A-frame addition which doubled his working space. In the center of the room, a tree grows straight up through the skylighted ceiling; John didn't have the heart to cut the tree down, so instead built around it. In front of the tree stands a wing-backed rattan throne, which fits in well with the raku urns and ceramic drums that line one wall. In the summer, the heat of the kiln makes the place an oven; in winter, John works with a space heater at his feet. He says he frequently spends 12 hours a day in the studio, but that it's by no means an oppressive thing. "The only time it gets tough is when there's real deadline. Then you might be spending 12 hours glazing some things where you'd rather be throwing some pots, but that's the name of the game if you're going to be making a living at something — you can't do purely what you want. I've made some concessions and adjustments but they've been fine because the process is really what I enjoy."

The Crossroads

"There's a certain crossroad there," reflects John. "You take something you really like — your music, your art, whatever it is — and then decide that because people like your work, you'll make the big move. You quit your job and do it on your own and very quickly find out whether you can still be happy running it as a business, doing things because of what the market wants. Frankly, I know a lot of people who couldn't do it that way. They went back to a regular job to take the economic pressure off so they could do their art in their spare time with no commercial concessions."

John's strategy has been twofold. First, he created a product he could wholesale to gift shops: a large, hand-carved and hand-painted stein, depicting the majestic Colorado Rockies. By simply adding a logo for the gift shop, he had an item that would retail for $25. The next step was to find a buyer.

While still in a cast, John made a trip to Vail where he dropped in at a local gift shop with some samples. "The owner saw these mugs and saw the potential; all he wanted to know was how much and how many I could make. At the end of the day I had an order." Before long, John saw that wholesaling relieved him of a big part of the marketing burden, allowing him much more time for actually making pottery. Before, he had done a lot of one-man shows and craft fairs that had been very time consuming but relatively unprofitable. "The time efficiency of taking your work, having somebody order a gross or a dozen of these or three dozen of these is nice. You deliver them, you get a check and they deal with selling them. You spend most of your time making the things and less time marketing them or packing and unpacking things that may not sell."

The reason it all works is the quasi assembly line approach that Hansen has devised. "I generally do a batch of 10 or 12 at a time. It's fast; I'll take about a half hour to throw all ten of them. The trimming part will take another half hour. The carving is probably the most time-consuming part, since there's a lot of detail and I'm not using a machine like the wheel. It takes me an hour to do a half dozen or so. Glazing takes about an hour to do a batch of ten and the firing time works out to be about an hour. I figured out that it takes me roughly an hour to produce a finished stein and they wholesale for around $10." Obviously, these are not fine art, says John. This is "bread and butter" that allows him time and freedom to do the kinds of things he really enjoys.

"My favorite part of the work is actually throwing the pots. It's the part of the process where you create something out of nothing. You have the clay from the buckets which you wedge up into a ball that sudenly takes on a form. Watching the form take shape is the most gratifying part and for me, the most fun. On the wheel there's something — the process of the wheel turning, watching the form take shape — it's hypnotic and the time just flies. Plus I'm good at it and you can enjoy doing something you're good at.

"Clay is wonderful for using a lot of different skills. There's so many aspects to it: There's sculpture, there's chemistry and geology, the technical aspects of the kiln. It can embody so many skills that it's a great vehicle for someone who wants to try a lot of things. I'm better at some than others, but I like to try to do it all myself. If that whole thing can work, I think that's success."

Hansen sees two approaches to making a living. One way, he feels, is to "do something you may not like but that pays a lot, then take the money and enjoy your free time. A more direct approach is to do something you really enjoy and find a way to make it pay.

"I think success is not so much repeating something that works in order to make money, as it is expanding and learning from your work." John is the first to admit that success for him has meant compromise. Still, he's happy with the end result. "My compromise is turning out the numbers of these steins to make the sales that make the whole thing work. I've dealt with that and it's OK. It allows me, when the bills are paid and I've got some free time, to expand and do other more creative pieces. This pays the bills and I learn from it."

Zeroing in on a "High-End" Market:
Sheryl and Joe Koch

"We can do better than this," was the sentiment that started the Chesnik-Koch enterprise. Stained glass was just a hobby for Sheryl Koch when she persuaded her mother to tag along to a guild meeting in San Diego five years ago. Among the things passed around at the meeting was a kaleidoscope. "Everyone was oohing and ahhing," remembers Sheryl. "At first, we oohed and ahhed, too, but then we looked at the workmanship and saw that it was very crudely made. We just kind of looked at each other and said, 'We can come up with something better than this.'"

A simple concept, a kaleidoscope is basically a tube with two revolving wheels at one end; mirrors inside refract the light into an infinity of patterns. The artistry comes into play in the selection of materials and the quality of the workmanship. What the two women came up with was a kaleidoscope exquisitely made of polished brass. The two revolving wheels are set with German antique glass and the finest Brazilian agate, each stone hand selected for color, texture and crystal conformation. Each is signed and dated. No two are ever alike.

A Strategic Decision

"It's basically an adult toy, for the person who has everything," explains Joe. "We made a strategic business decision a couple of years ago to get into a business where we wouldn't have to worry about ups and downs in the economy." That meant going after a high-end clientele, people with lots of discretionary money to spend. "We sell to high-end shops throughout the country," he says. "By high-end I mean the MGM Grand Hotel in Las Vegas, Ghiaridelli Square in San Francisco, Samson Fine Arts in Cape Cod."

Of course, getting into these top drawer retail outlets wasn't a matter of merely picking up the phone. "You do a lot of walking," says Sheryl. "We'd load a bunch of kaleidoscopes in the car, box them up and put them underneath our arms and walk into the store. We'd always go for the best store in town. We'd decide on our first, second and third choices and then go see if they'd be interested." Now that the business is well established, the bulk of their sales comes from phone reorders. While Joe declines to name a figure, he will say that the business has been "extremely lucrative."

Excellence: The Real High

"Quality is the most important thing," says Sheryl. "If we don't have our quality we don't have our business." As Joe points out, the rewards for quality sometimes come from unexpected sources: "You get a call from a customer," and he says, 'Guess who just walked into our store and bought a kaleidoscope.' Hal Linden bought three; Ron Howard got a Tripod; Marlon Brando bought eight."

Or, says Sheryl, "I walked into my gynecologist's office and there was one of my kaleidoscopes sitting on his desk. That was really something — he didn't know I made it." Did she tell him? "Of course!"

Expansion Through Teaching: Charlotte Elich-McCall

"One thing that has helped me survive," says Charlotte of her 7-year-old operation, "is keeping my business overhead down. Like this location: It's not a high-rent area, but it has the charm of what I do. People find me. And because we did all the work remodeling the building we got six months free rent from the owner." Even after that first six months, the rent remained very reasonable. "My first lease was for three years and each year it went up a very small amount — sometimes only $10 a year."

Another contributing factor, Charlotte feels, has been the growth generated by offering crafts classes in the store. "When I first opened I had a weaving class, a crochet class and a spinning class. I think that over a period of time the classes create a clientele. I still see people that I taught seven years ago. Because they learned here, they keep coming back.

"All my teachers are contract labor. When I first started I taught all the weaving classes and the spinning class, and had one other woman who taught the crochet class. As we grew, just talking with people as they came in I discovered others who could teach and just asked them if they'd be interested in teaching here. Now I have 16 women teaching different classes."

Specializing: Elton Norwood, Antique Restoration

"I took on this work for my own personal perfection," says Elton Norwood, a slight, soft-spoken man in his fifties with a profound appreciation for the craftsmanship of pre-industrial societies. "Most of us think we're such hot stuff in the twentieth century — we ain't so hot. I've got a little bird box made in 1780 that's as intricate as anything you'd ever want to see. All made by hand. Very few people in this country could make such a thing today." Restoring these pieces, he says, is an exacting test of both technical skill and personal discipline.

"The thing I like most about this work is that there's nothing to hide behind," says Norwood. "Either the music is there or it isn't." His current project has been a remarkable feat of mental stamina. The large music box, almost the size of a small bathtub, belongs to the president of a cosmetics company; already Norwood has spent "a ton of hours" on it. The box is beautiful. Still, he points out, outward appearances are the least of the problems. Getting music out of its 11 cylinders is the true test of craftsmanship. "When you get a job like this you've got to be a detective. You've got to run down all the things that have happened to the piece. Look for all the telltale signs, the file marks, the places where it's been re-nickel plated. Try to figure out why there are 14 teeth broken out of the comb.

A Work of Perfection

"The songs may sound simple, but they're not. Some pieces are so complex you can listen to them 20 times and still hear new melodies. You cut your teeth on the simple boxes, then you get the big, complex cylinders that may be 16 inches long and 4 in diameter, playing something like Rossini's overtures — not simple at all. Moving a pin just a thousandth of an inch is critical. A half a thousandth will show in the music — 20 thousandths is like a football field. Getting that kind of accuracy is very, very difficult and the thrill is getting it just right. It's a work of perfection.

"In this work you'd better do each step as perfectly as you can because your attention span is only so long; you don't want to have to go back and do a thing over again. If you're regulating 10,000 pins you could be there until Dooms Day." Fooling with the delicate pins is risky, he adds. "The metal doesn't have that much life that you can bend the pins around. You've got to get them right the first time around or they start breaking on you."

He continues enthusiastically, "It requires great focus of concentration. I didn't know this when I started, but eventually the individual, rather than the music box, becomes the instrument. Your focus builds. I can focus intensely on a cylinder for two or three hours straight without getting up. Ten years ago I could never have done that, but I can now.

"I like that focus because I can use it for other things. I can solve problems because I can focus my attention on something long enough to get the answer. It's given me patience, taught me humility. You learn not to get ticked off because you can't throw the thing. In order to do this work you have to maintain a certain sense of peace within yourself."

Becoming a Part of History

Norwood's respect for craftsmanship is apparent as he describes the building process. "With a really fine box, you can figure 15 or 20 people worked on it when it was first made. The brass was pricked first, probably by a woman, then drilled, then somebody put the pins in and justified them. Women did this because of the delicate manual skill they have. Men cut the combs out and had all the factory parts cast. It was a group effort.

"When I restore a piece it becomes, in a sense, mine. It's a dead horse when it gets here — restorable junk. Then you give it life once more and it's good for another 150 years. I've warmed the steel with the heat of my hands; I've embued this whole thing with my essence. Along with all the other people who've ever worked on this piece, I'm part of the history of the box now."

"Do the Best You Can . . . Then Do Better"

The cosmetics company president will pay almost $14,000 for the restored music box, an effort that will have taken Norwood almost a year. This project will be only one of about 50 he'll do this year. A member of the national association for music box restorers, his customers seek him out from all over the country. There is now a 2-1/2-year waiting list for his services.

Although the work is solitary, Norwood says he works with a sense of obligation to his fellows. "Do the best you can, and when you think that's good enough, do better. Work as though everybody in the music box society were looking over your shoulder, because in truth they are. When you send a piece like this out, it's an advertisement. People in the society are all over this country and Europe, as close as the telephone. They're going to see that box; if they like what they see, it's good talk. If it's not good work, you get lousy word of mouth. I could have gotten away with shoddy work when I first started because I worked with an antique dealer who said, 'Listen, three-fourths of the people aren't going to know the difference anyway.' I said, 'But I know the difference.' I'm a musician and I can hear the difference. I can't live with that. I like to go to bed at night feeling good about myself."

Then there are the times he sees the impact his best work has upon the music box owner. "We finished up a music box once for an old man — his grandfather had won it in a raffle and had passed it on. He had heard this music box his whole life with all the squeaks and all the problems. It was worn out by the time he brought it to me. When we restored it we played it for him and he was so thrilled he actually danced. To see this man just come alive was a real thrill. When you fix a music box that's been in somebody's family a long time, you're touching their emotions. You're restoring their memories, giving them back something very special. That's worth a lot."

Kay Casperson, Mime

There is probably no occupation so surrounded by the glamour mystique as that of performing artist — musicians, dancers, actors. Whether it's perpetuated by press agents or the artists themselves is hard to say, but the result of all the hype is an illusion in the public's mind that performing is one continuous peak experience, a never-ending cast party. The truth is that performing is basically hard work — often boring, sometimes grueling — punctuated by occasional peak, ecstatic experiences that sustain the artist through all the rest.

Kay Casperson started dancing at 17; at 40, she is a veteran of 23 years. She explains her abiding love for performing. "On the one-to-one thing, I'm very shy, but put me out in front of 3,000 people and (snapping her fingers) I'll do anything. I am first and foremost a performer. I mean, gee, if you can get 300 people to love you at the same time — it's exciting."

The Humor/Healing Connection

"When I got out of school in the mid-sixties, there were a lot of things that still weren't happening for women. I realized that as a female psychologist, I was going to end up running rats through mazes for somebody else. So when I auditioned for a modern jazz dance company and was given a chance to join, I took it. I started dancing and liked it a lot — forgot all about psychology. From there I was cast in a musical. I could sing and dance, I found, but I couldn't act my way out of a paper bag. I thought the problem was that I'd never studied, but when I started studying acting I realized the real hangup was that I couldn't move and speak at the same time. The logical thing was to study mime. That worked. So I got into legitimate theater and have been doing it ever since.

"The connection between my psych background and clowning isn't as obscure as one would think," reflects Kay. "It's sort of funny: A lot of clowns are sociologists. There's that healing thing in humor. As a psych major I went to (two mental health facilities) quite a bit and worked with disturbed teenagers to see if there was something I could do. As I started working with them, I realized that I could gain their trust by entertaining them with tricks, music, juggling, magic.

"I love doing the school programs, seeing those seas of 500 little faces. They're blown away," she laughs. "After all, they seldom see a real classical clown; what they see is Ronald McDonald." One big reward for Kay is seeing children's growing awareness of the arts. "There is much greater appreciation for the arts in public schools today than in the past. Ten years ago I wouldn't have had the staff support in the schools because educators didn't realize the need. Now they're saying, 'Get in here and work with these kids.'

"I once had a wonderful experience at a camp for deaf children. It was really early in my career as a mime and I had been booked there by an arts council. I had never performed for deaf people so my first reaction was 'I can't go work with those kids; I don't even know sign language,' but they sent me anyway and gave me an interpreter so if something wasn't clear to the kids they could ask her. Through that experience I realized that people who don't hear have a different sense of humor. Everything is real visual to them; their humor was much simpler but much more sophisticated at the same time. They reacted to psychological humor rather than verbal humor.

"It changed the way I thought about my work. I realized that even though I was a mime, a silent performer, I was really gearing my work to language. I thought, 'Here I am working silent, with gesture, and I don't know anything about real silence.' That was a real breakthrough for me."

Getting Started: Staying Booked

"I started out by doing shows and workshops for the arts councils," recalls Kay. "I was an independent contractor; if they had a big street festival, I'd do roving things. In fact, that's how I developed the masks. There was never a big enough budget to hire a big cast of people, so we would use a few people who could change into lots of different characters. I started making these huge masks just to keep warm in the winter streets.

"Then one of the symphony orchestra conductors saw me performing as a mime in one of these shows and said, 'Gee, this is wonderful. Come do it with the orchestra.' That's how I got involved in the symphony shows. Then another orchestra would hire me. If you can stick with something long enough, people hear about you.

"The problem is working on you own, being an independent contractor; it's so shaky at first that lots of people give up the boat. Part of it is just sticking it out. There are times when there is just no money coming in. I've been able to freelance because as a kid I learned a lot of things and I've kept learning. Like I'm not a *great* musician, but I can play music. I'm not a great mime, but being a jack-of-all-trades has been the thing that's helped me survive." One week it might be an October street festival; during the school year Kay performs for grade schoolers; in summer there will be the outdoor symphony concerts, and in between, the mall openings and the cocktail parties.

"I just want to keep working," says Kay. "You know, even though I prefer doing a stage show with the symphony, if somebody's going to pay me $150 an hour to appear at their cocktail party. . . . I basically try to do the best I can in any situation.

"I really like not having people telling me what to do. I'd hate to get in the position where there was so much pressure — like in a big show — where it started interfering with what I consider my artistic prowess. I feel enough pressure doing it by myself."

Maintaining the Instrument

What's the hardest part? "Keeping the energy up," replies Kay. "Making myself rehearse by myself. It's more fun to practice with other people. Staying fit is hard, too. Doing the jogging, staying on the diet." At this, she shoots an evil glance at her half-empty glass of light beer, scolding herself in stage whisper, "Beer!

"I try to watch my diet but I'm not terribly careful about it. The years I was a dancer I was smoking a pack of cigarettes and eating two candy bars a day. You don't realize when you're younger that if you maintain it early it will stay longer." Her preferred weight is "always ten pounds less than where I am. Even at my skinniest I still wanted to be skinnier. It's not a vanity thing as much as it is just energy. The more weight you have off the more energy you have for movement."

"You Have All These Expectations"

Kay admits that as a young dancer, she, like her peers, had dreams of fame and fortune. "I expected to go to New York and become a Broadway star," she says, "but when I got to New York I hated living there and I was too short to be a dancer. It was pre-Twyla Tharp and you had to be 5'7" to get into any chorus line in any musical. I knew that I wanted to pursue the arts, but I also knew that I wanted to have kids and some sort of normalcy in my life. I didn't want to commit everything to the theater." She and her husband, Jack, an actor, are the parents of two teenagers.

"I'm glad now that I didn't put all my pennies in the same bucket. Besides, I'm not so sure I haven't enjoyed most of the same payoffs without the incredible pressures. I really love my time in the studio, creating new pieces, designing new masks. I've made all the masks myself — thousands of them. With the masks, even though I'm a one-person show, I'm really eight characters."

Kay's studio is behind the house in a large, open-raftered garage which has been divided into two long, spacious rooms. The larger room is oak floored, with 2' x 6' sections of mirror against one wall. In one corner sits a jerry-rigged sound system made from a tape player and small radio speakers. Portable, this is the self-contained sound system Kay takes on jobs. The other room is filled with masks of all sizes and descriptions. This garage studio has worked out perfectly for Kay. It allows her to be on hand if her children need supervision, but also gives her a space to work "where they aren't."

While many performers feel that star status is absolutely essential to success, Kay obviously doesn't agree. She has found tremendous satisfaction in the quieter, perhaps more balanced lifestyle she prefers. "I have a real good friend that I grew up with and danced with and went off to New York with. She travels all over the world now, choreographing for American Ballet Theater, but her marriage has collapsed. You have to be very self-centered to survive on that level of pressure and stress. You must have a vision.

"I have a vision, and I believe I can accomplish the things I want to do, it just takes longer. Twenty-three years," she muses. "I could have done it in less time, but there have been times when I've wanted to take the summer off and take the kids camping; times when I didn't want to perform. This has been the right road for me."

The Collectors

"Having this gallery was just a vision, a dream that I decided to make come true."

Joan Robey

Collectors such as gallery owners, antique dealers, and book and art dealers often have reasons for going into business that make profit almost beside the point. Joan Robey is an example. One look at her sleek apartment will tell you that her gallery is, in truth, a moneymaking avocation, the logical outgrowth of a lifelong passion for collecting. Everywhere there are exquisite examples of what Joan calls "contemporary crafts": handblown glass, wood and ceramic sculpture. On the fireplace mantle rests a gorgeous piece of pink and cream garbage-fired clay, and a fabulous woolen mountain sheep stands near the window next to a century-old cactus. "I've always been wildly attracted to beautiful things," Joan explains, unnecessarily. Remove the dining room table and her home itself might be a gallery. Why, then, has Joan gone to the trouble of opening a store?

First, she replies, she wanted to start her own business. She knew it would be some kind of retail store and what better merchandise to deal in than something she already knew and loved? Although her own professional background had been in business rather than fine art, "it's always been something I've played with. As a kid I used to make things. In the sixties I lived in San Francisco; I worked on a wood lathe, making dolls and things." Robey says that operating the gallery, deciding what will be shown and how it will be shown, has become her own creative outlet. "In the gallery I'm trying to go for the small space where contemporary crafts and fine art meet. It's an incredible thrill surrounding myself with things I consider fulfilling and beautiful. I see in the artwork the artist's struggle expressing himself. I can't do it, but owning this gallery is my way of being an artist."

Though the collectors in this chapter are unquestionably business people, they all name rewards other than money as their primary motivators. Profits allow them to live comfortably but the real satisfactions, they say, come from finding and acquiring new treasures, from learning and sharing with other collectors.

COLLECTING: THE MEANS AND THE END

"You know, we're in the greatest recycling business in the world," remarks antique dealer Pauli Wanderer, a wren-like woman in her early fifties. "I've loved old things ever since I was a child and although I believe in preserving the past, I really love these things just for themselves." For instance, "I wouldn't think of refinishing this," she says, pointing to the pine work table that serves as kitchen dinette. Built around 1850, the table is scarred and dented, its once-varnished surface dulled to a soft patina by generations of elbows resting upon it. In Pauli's eyes, every nick enhances its appeal.

"Obviously I Love it, Fool That I Am!"

"Most dealers are collectors," says Pauli. "I have a friend who's in the business simply to augment her personal collection. She buys and sells and works very hard at it, but it's really to augment what she has in her own house. She's always on the lookout and when she finds something wonderful, she keeps it."

"I really don't have that much compared to some of my friends," Pauli says. Her house, a rambling sprawl of rooms thrown against a wooded hillside, contains a hodgepodge of furniture and relics that run the gamut from Chippendale to folk art. Pauli darts about, pulling this plate and that vase from shelves and cupboards. From her kitchen window sill she takes a Majolica plate found at a flea market. "This is an acquired taste," she allows, noting the garish glaze. "To look at it, you'd never guess it was worth anything." True enough.

Pauli Wanderer
Uncle Sam's Antiques

From a shelf over the stove she hands down a lovely old yellow ware bread bowl; resting inside is a well-used wooden potato masher. Over the entrance to the breakfast nook hangs a dilapidated bait sign, cut from a 1 x 12 plank into the shape of a fish. This piece of folk art Pauli salvaged from a fishing dock in Wisconsin; it is her prized possession.

Her store, a barnish structure dubbed "Uncle Sam's Country Antiques," boasts an ever varying array of vintage furniture and housewares: handmade hunting decoys, maple and cherry Boston rockers, circa 1830; quilts dating from the 1860s, iron beds and pine workbenches, a country secretary picked up in Wisconsin. Jelly cupboards, harvest tables, rag rugs — the very names evoke visions of pioneers and rural housewives and most of all, a simpler time, a more fundamental culture.

"Obviously, I love it, fool that I am!" Pauli exclaims, wondering if she hasn't subconsciously set out to create a heritage for herself. "These candlesticks I bought when my daughter was born 15 years ago. They were handmade in the 1830s." She laughs, remembering how excited she was to get them. "I bought them for myself as a reward for having that baby."

Donna Hudgel, Trails West Book Store

"There was no way to control my interest in the West," explains Donna Hudgel. "Some people can zero in on a topic like mining or the Custer Battle, but I was all over, into everything — couldn't stop. I thought, 'Gee, there's more books out there than I'll ever be able to own. What better way to satisfy my collecting impulse than to have a book store?'" Hudgel's book store, "Trails West," is a testament to her fascination with western Americana. On the wall behind the desk a leather Indian ceremonial dress is displayed along with several watercolors and oils depicting cowboys. Across the room a huge string of dried chilis hangs next to a bronze statue of a cutting horse and its rider. A wood-wheeled buckboard, draped with saddle blankets and old horse tack, dominates one half of the store; underneath the wagon lies a bleached horse skull. The floor-to-ceiling, wall-to-wall bookshelves are packed with volumes on more topics than one can imagine, everything from the expected *Lewis and Clark Among the Indians* and *Jim Bowie's Lost Mine* to such unlikely titles as *Pioneer Jews* and *Saloons of the American West*. There are books about Kit Carson and Molly Brown, as well as *The Unabridged Jack London* and *A Guide for the Alaskan Prospector*.

This amazing selection of titles suggests one explanation for Donna's enduring interest in the West: the genre encompasses a nearly endless variety of topics. That's it exactly, confirms Hudgel. "Western Americana is limited only by the geographic lines of the western continental United States. Pick a subject," she challenges. "Art, music, literature, exploration, crime, romance, politics, industry — there isn't a subject that can't be applied to the West in one manner or another."

Sharing Information and Experiences

"I have wondered if this is the only business where the proprietor of the store learns more from the customers than the customers learn from the proprietor, because each customer, within his field, is an expert. He has read the 150 books on his subject — on mining, let's say. The next guy, he's into Custer and he's read 2,000 books on Custer. Certainly I haven't read that many books on it all."

The thing that is beautiful, Donna feels, is the sharing of information and experiences. "As readily and easily as young people bring in their new babies and show them off, people my age bring in their mothers and their dads or their grandmothers and grandfathers, and the stories go. Somebody brings her mother who's visiting from New Mexico. She's 80 years old and she remembers when [some famous outlaw] used to pass through their ranch. I feel like I'm meeting a celebrity — I mean this person was *there*. That happens often and it's part of the excitement."

Richard Schwartz, Stage House II Books

Richard Schwartz is possessed of tremendous energy and drive. Bright, articulate, he might at one time have been shy, but any reticence has long since been lost in his enthusiasm for his work. His story is an intriguing rollercoaster ride of struggle, triumph, loss and recovery, held together by determination and commitment to an idea. Another factor in his ultimate success might have been his becoming, at last, reconciled with his own devotion to "the printed word."

"I think the book represents tradition to a lot of pepole. They're frightfully in awe of computers, the whole modern technological revolution. They're afraid of the accumulating unknowns in their lives. They find security by reaching back into the past: This was good for my father, it used to be good for me."

Interestingly enough, Schwartz' entrepreneurial story began with a jail stretch. "I was drafted out of graduate school during the Vietnam era," he says.

Richard Schwartz
Stage House II Books

"I joined the navy and spent four and a half years on an aircraft carrier in the Mediterranean." He had pursued a liberal arts degree at Johns Hopkins, but recalls that his social life consisted mainly of sit-ins and protests that eventually landed him in jail. When his student deferments ran out he enlisted, and was dismayed to find out that because of the restrictions posed by his police record, he was relegated to maintenance work. It turned out not to be so bad. He was trained as an electrician and loved it; would have spent his tour in the service contentedly working on generators if his outfit hadn't been assigned to duty in Vietnam. This time his protest took the form of jumping ship and Schwartz quickly found himself in jail again with lots of time to think.

While still a student he had lived with his parents in a room over his mother's antique shop. A scholarly kid, he had persuaded his mother to hold on to some of the steady supply of used books that flowed in along with the antiques; the books were stored out back in a barn. It was while he was maintaining engines on the aircraft carrier that the idea first came to him that what his hometown needed was a good used book store. He kept his idea on a back burner until the monotony of jail forced him to think seriously about what he would finally end up doing for a living. "I thought, if I had this used book store I could sit and read all the time, write and converse with intelligent people . . . it would be a very wonderful existence and I'd probably make a lot of money too. These are the kinds of crazy, idiotic thoughts you have when you're in prison or down in a generator room eight decks below the water line."

Despite this self-effacement, Schwartz knew his idea was neither crazy nor idiotic, and decided to write to his father, a retired architect, to ask for advice. "I didn't expect him to take me too seriously but lo and behold, when I got home from the navy, he had already leased an old garage and started converting it into a neat little book store. He put in shelves and stocked the place with books from a porno shop that had been busted. My mother had sold the antique shop and there were still all those used books out in the barn. I salvaged the best of those and brought them to the store. That was my beginning. From that a really thriving book business developed." At 27, Schwartz was an entrepreneur.

The Challenge of Expansion

"What happens when you're in a used merchandise business is you're constantly being offered things other than what you sell. People would bring in prints — Currier and Ives, Audubon prints, you name it." At first,

Schwartz says, he rejected the idea: "Oh! I'm a book dealer. I can't deal in this sort of thing." But then he recognzied that there was also a demand for prints. "I also realized, having done a modicum of research by that time, that the print is the child of the book. All the great early prints really sprang from books."

Next it was paintings, and before long the business was booming, "grossing a half million" in its best year. I had a fairly large payroll, four employees and a manager. The art business increased to the point that I took on a minor partnership in a gallery in Munich. I was spending a lot of time over in Germany, buying things here and selling them over there. We bought out the dance studio overhead — a move that expanded our place from 1,800 square feet to 4,000. We had a wonderful gallery upstairs, had a couple of art shows which really helped the business. Things worked almost too well.

Some five years ago, things started to come apart. With the combined pressures of the business and a pending divorce, Schwartz grew "increasingly alcoholic." The final blow came when he learned from his banker that he'd been the victim of a major embezzlement. "I was in Germany and my checks started to bounce. Impossible! It was inconceivable to me that somebody could be spending my money, but there it was. . . ."

"In a sense I deserved it. I was too abstracted from the business, too arrogant about it. I'd been thinking, 'I'm a highfalutin' art dealer. I'm an expert in rare and antiquarian prints and I don't need the ma and pa type of people off the streets. I don't need Mr. Everyman coming in asking me for a copy of *God and the Groceryman*. It was this pulling myself away from the real center of the business where I think I made my big mistake. At any rate, the result of all this was I sold my lease and I was nowhere for four or five months. I was just drunk."

Starting Over

Today, Stage House II is once more a thriving concern, two stories of alcoves containing irresistibly time-worn volumes: first editions of Oscar Wilde's *Salome*, Melville's *White Jacket*, Thoreau's *Walden*. Mark Twain, Robert Frost, Errol Flynn; an autographed collection of Ansel Adams photographs, a vintage Elvis Presley album. There is a steady flow of traffic from the sidewalk — a woman bringing in a cookbook to sell — as well as the out-of-state customer who comes to the store once every three years.

"When I picked myself up, I picked myself up in debt to the tune of about $20,000," says Schwartz. "This business has managed to pay off those debts but it's taken about $100,000 to develop the business to what it is now."

He took on a partner, "a customer who had been a book scout for the Salvation Army. I'd known George for a long time. I'd tried to form partnerships with a couple of other dealers in town but they turned me down. Thought I was a worthless wreck, a terrible business person. George had nothing to lose by going into busienss with me, plus we liked each other a lot."

The two men started out on an ultra-modest scale, gathering up some of Schwartz's remaining stock to sell at book fairs. Sales were so good they were encouraged to lease "this little bitty niche in the theatre building. About 400 square feet and dusty as hell. We didn't prosper but we did alright." After six months, however, their landlords kicked them out, a blessing in disguise, says Schwartz. It forced them to look for much-needed space.

They settled on a location that had been a Divine Light mission headquarters. "We were attracted to the place for one reason: it had a lot of traffic. We wanted to try a high-traffic location, which absolutely flies in the face of standard used book store theory which says, get a quiet, off-street, low-rent location and develop a destination trade. What we had found in these book fairs was that the book can attract impulse buyers. People who hadn't come to buy a book would pass by and if the price was right, they'd buy. We said let's go for it. We gutted the building, built a mezzanine and cubicles for books. As soon as we opened, we started to make money selling books, so the whole process started over again, only on a higher, more energetic level. We service a huge, disparate market — everything from free books to $10,000 books. Everything from cheap little book prints to $100,000 paintings. We've sold a painting for $80,000 out of that damned store, and quite a few for $5,000 to $15,000.

"Once, when I was really down, when George and I were just starting this new business, I applied to Western Disposal to work on the back of a garbage truck. I even went to the trouble to get some good references. But they turned me down. He didn't believe I would stay with it. He knew that I would regard it as a temporary job. So he hired some other guy and that guy's still with him, enjoying life." Schwartz leans back in his chair and laughs heartily.

THE SEARCH: "THE INHERENT PAYOFF"

Next to actually owning the objects, the process of searching for and finding collectibles is probably the most exciting part of the business. It's not easy though; this kind of detective work demands a sharp eye and a bloodhound's instincts, as well as a certain amount of luck — simply being in the right place at the right time.

"I've always got my eye pealed," says Pauli Wanderer, "and now that I'm in this business I *have* to keep my eye pealed. For one thing, your shop has to look different all the time. If it doesn't change, nobody comes back. The problem for antique dealers is we can't just go to the merchandise mart and order something. People will come in and say, 'When are you going to get another cherry table?' or 'We want a black rag doll, when are you going to get another one?' Nobody delivers in this business. We have to go out and look for it."

On the other hand, Pauli will be the first to admit, while searching for new inventory is essential to survival, the detective work involved is also a big part of the fun, especially when one comes upon a great find. "We all enjoy the excitement of the search. You never know where you're going to find something wonderful. Just the process of scanning over piles and piles of dust-covered junk in garage sales and flea markets and coming up with something you find beautiful is very rewarding. In fact, I would have to say that the search is *the* inherent payoff of the business."

Every Trip a Business Trip

"I've always loved to travel — I'll travel at the drop of a hat," says Pauli. Good thing, because searching for additions to one's stock often means many miles on the road. For collectors like Richard Schwartz, combing the countryside for buys is just one of the built-in enjoyments of the business. "One of the great things about being a book and art dealer is that you're basically a prospector," says Schwartz, whose prospecting takes him to places like Kansas City, El Paso and San Francisco. "There's nothing more exciting than being out on the road and going into junk shops, antique shops, peoples' homes, looking for good stuff."

Joan Robey, who also admits to being a bit of a travel bug, says, "I probably take half a dozen trips a year to different cities — New York, San Francisco — last year I went to Italy. I go to craft shows, art shows, other galleries, really searching for artwork. I have gone to shows and looked at virtually a thousand artists' work in order to find eight or ten whose work I want in my gallery." Being a collector, Joan says, lends an added sense of purpose to her visits. "It used to be that when I would travel, one of the things I loved to do was to go to the galleries. Now I do the same thing, only I write it off.

"There's definitely an ego thing that comes with it too," she observes. "I don't do any national advertising, so I'm not necessarily nationally known, but because I've shown artists' work from different parts of the country, the Robey-Slabeck Gallery name has gotten around somewhat. In November I was in Philadelphia and went into a gallery there. When I introduced myself to the owner of the gallery she said, 'Oh, I've heard very nice things about your gallery.' What could be nicer than to have that kind of recognition?"

"It's exciting meeting artists," says Kathe MacLaren, "and with us we have a special thing that happens." The special thing Kathe refers to is the immense enjoyment she and her partner, Joan, both take from traveling and from just being together. Wherever they go, she says, the two carry on an animated dialogue, talking and laughing nonstop, plainly having a wonderful time. Other people just naturally gravitate toward them. Because they are a pair, people seem much less hesitant to approach the two of them than they would a single woman; perceived as a livening addition, they are frequently invited to artists' homes for parties. Seeing famous artists in their own homes has been an eye opener, says Kathe. "Part of the glamour people associate with meeting artists is the idea that they're so untouchable when in fact, many of them are just down-to-earth, wonderful people."

Another idea common among outsiders is that the business of collecting is a little cloak-and-daggerish, fraught with cut-throat competition among dealers. These collectors say that hasn't been the case. "I think we all help each other," says Pauli. "I often call a dealer and say, 'Someone just offered me some wicker and I don't sell wicker. Should she call you?' I send other dealers a lot of customers."

Donna Hudgel agrees. "My husband is continually amazed at how well book dealers get along with one another, as opposed to carpet dealers, where it's a little bit of a cut-throat world. I think book people are just among the greatest people in the world. They're active, they're involved, and people who are like this just naturally share. If I have a book and I don't know what it is and I ask a dealer whether he's seen it, he is very happy to share this information with me because he knows that next week, he's going to have a book that he's never seen before and maybe I know something about it. It's easy for the camaraderie to be there. Our love for what we're doing just naturally pours out."

DARE I TAKE THIS RISK?

Can laying one's artistic soul on the line, struggling to communicate one's passion for something to an unaware public be called anything so simple as "consumer education"? For Joan Robey, laying her tastes before the public has represented the ultimate risk. "You really have to have your determination intact," she warns. "I did, but still there was a great internal struggle over '*dare* I take this risk?' I mean, you put your ass on the line, whether it's your financial ass or your tastes, your personality." Think about it, she continues, "people are often aftraid to buy a piece of art to hang on their wall because they're afraid their friends are going to walk into their house and say, 'I can't *believe* they did this.' Well, the gallery is like taking all of my taste and putting it out there."

Joan recalls that she overcame her fears of rejection by asking herself what, truly, was the worst thing that could happen. "I went through the scenario of having my grand opening party and having no one show up. I imagined that and asked myself whether I would be able to survive. And my answer was, 'Well, I will probably be able to get up the next morning and go on.' At that point I was totally committed."

Richard Schwartz remembers his own struggle with public awareness. "When I started out one of the most frustrating problems I had was convincing people that a used book was worth something more than a quarter. I mean I couldn't stand this thing of saying, 'Look, this is the *printed word.* The pages might be worn, but it is a book — something of value.' I fought this educational war with people for a long time."

As others have pointed out, often the only thing needed to make a good idea profitable is time. After a four-year hiatus from "the street-level, walk-in book business," Schwartz returned to find that a drastic change in attitude had taken place. "George and I did these book fairs, took these used books and put them up on dilapidated shelves in a booth next to a potter on one side and a stained glass vendor on the other. I was astounded at peoples' response — it was absolutely antithetical to what it had been." Schwartz remembers customers pulling down great armfuls of books and asking "Is this the real price? Are these really $3?" "Yeah," Schwartz would growl, ready to put on the gloves and slug it out. He was dumbstruck when the person would exclaim, "Great! I'll take this and this and this. . . . "

TREATING THE CUSTOMER GENTLY

The same principles involved in mass consumer education also hold true for individuals. With patient nurturing and a genuine concern on the part of the dealer, a customer who's only tentatively interested can become an enthusiastic collector himself. Joan Robey observes, "People will often not buy something the first time they see it, even though they do like it. They often have to come back and see it again and learn more about it and develop confidence that they will like it in their own home. Sometimes it's frustrating dealing with people's fears of their own inadequacy. Sometimes I feel like a shrink because of how I see people bound up in thinking, 'Oh, what will my friends say if I put that piece on my table?' I have to gently encourage them by saying 'It's okay. If you like, go ahead and allow yourself the chance to do it.'

"It's a matter of my being there — or the gallery being there so the person can come back the next month and the next, each time getting more of a sense of what's going on. My being willing to talk to that person helps him feel more comfortable and eventually he will come back and buy. But that means you've got to have staying power. The business is not going to pop open and be brilliant the first year. You probably won't make any money even in the second year."

But once it all comes together, the shop has developed a consistent clientele, there's a steady flow of new inventory, customers provide an ongoing stimulating exchange of information and experiences — once this happens, the business can be the happiest of endeavors. Joan Markowitz describes one of her favorite experiences: "We had one young man come in who had never collected before. His first purchase was a soup turreen. Two years later he bought a beautiful Miró aquatint. This is so exciting for us — it's something brand new for them and it becomes something exciting and enriching that they go on to do. Suddenly, they open magazines and they're aware; now when they go on vacation they look at art. We've had people bring in things they've bought on their trips — they want to share them with us."

MAKING A CONTRIBUTION

"I could never have a store that didn't really do what I needed to do," remarks Joan Robey. "I couldn't sell knickknacks — I wouldn't feel I was making a contribution." Joan frowns slightly as she tries to articulate her most basic reasons for conducting her business the way she does. "I definitely feel I have a mission. You look at things that are going on that are really important in the world, like people starving and you say, 'Where does this mission of presenting contemporary crafts as fine art fit in?' I mean, if you want to do something that's 'mission-ful,' why don't you feed the starving people of Africa? But I think the quality of life is what makes life worthwhile. I mean, you get up, you go to work every day — there's got to be those moments. For me, it's that sense of joy that comes from offering something that I think is beautiful and worthy to people."

MONEY MYTHS

There clearly are some good reasons for making a career of collecting; unfortunately, people sometimes launch stores and galleries with aims that aren't necessarily bad, but *are* probably ill-founded. Some are drawn to art or antique dealerships by unrealistic notions about the profits involved. Too often, these people are disappointed by the realities of the trade. "If I've learned nothing else, it's that the top line means nothing." says Joan Markowitz. "Let's say someone tells me they did $1 million last year. I say 'Great!' But did it cost you $1.5 million to do that?' People look at a painting that sells for $4,000 and say, 'Gee, you're going to get rich on that.' No, we're not going to get rich — we're going to get a percentage, but we'll have to work very hard for it."

One thing to consider is that collecting is by nature an inventory-intensive business. Selling things on consignment helps, of course, but that type of arrangement is not always available to the dealer who's just starting out. "When I first opened," says Joan Robey, "I bought virtually everything because I didn't have much of a relationship with the artists whose work I was selling. Now it's a little easier to get work on consignment, but I still do own a lot of inventory. That's hard because the money that's sitting in your pots and glass and jewelry is money you can't use for anything else."

Misconceptions About Markup

"One common misconception is that dealers pick up fantastic finds for nothing and then sell at huge profits, getting rich by cheating old ladies," remarks Pauli Wanderer. "The truth is I'm often supporting old ladies by buying things I might have to sell at a loss. I could never cheat an old lady who comes in needing to sell. I think most dealers are the same way."

Matters of Conscience

"There are matters of conscience in everything you do, whether you're buying or selling," states Richard Schwartz. "You have to confront your own conscience all the time and it's strictly you. You're not in a slot of management where you can sort of pass the buck on, or even drop the buck at five o'clock.

"A long time ago there was a great old gal named Jenny Curtis. She was one of these typical junk ladies — she just thrived on junk and her *mode de vivre* was to collect stuff for her grandchildren. She brought me a couple of really old, rare books, printed in the 1700s. At the time, she was a little irrational and she was in distress so I gave her $20 for them. Well, I sold them within two days for a couple hundred. First off I had this incredible thrill because I'd made a lot of money. But it just got me down. I could not rationalize — as much as I tried over the next few days — the amount of money I had paid Jenny compared with what I'd made on the books. So I went out and started drinking and at the end of that drinking bout, I realized that I had to do something about it. I went to Jenny and tried to give her more money. I said, 'Jenny, I made a lot of money on those books. I've got another $75 that I want to give you.' She wouldn't take it. She went on and on about something irrelevant and I realized that she had closed that particular chapter of her life. Finally, I went to her husband, Percy, and just pressed the money on him. I stuffed the money in his pocket and said, 'Percy, this is money for Jenny for the books I sold.' I don't know whether the money ever actually got back to Jenny, but I felt just slightly better after that, and I resolved to myself never to do that again."

Of course, not everyone who brings in a rare book or a painting to a dealer is irrational; some are dealers themselves who can well afford to part with an item. In that case, business is business, right? "In the art business," explains Schwartz, "if you make an enormous profit on something generally you get caught. The art business is so small and the number of real art buyers is so small that it's like a club. If you pay $10,000 for a painting and sell it for $1 million there're going to be 16 guys in there suing you, attaching your profits on one pretext or another.

"Sometimes I will make as much as seven or eight times my money — often you can do that inadvertently because you buy a collection and make a price on it without realizing there's something in the collection that's a lot more valuable than you thought it was — but right now the standard in the trade is you triple your money. If you pay $3 for a book you pretty well have to get $8 or $9 for it."

COLLECTORS ANONYMOUS

"People can't stop buying books any more than they can stop placing bets or drinking."

Donna Hudgel

Just mention the word "addiction" and dealers will nod and smile knowingly, almost as if a certain degree of compulsiveness were the earmark of a true collector. Joan Markowitz remembers one man who certainly qualifies. "This fellow came into the gallery on a Saturday. We had just come back from a major museum show down in Santa Fe and we were talking and talking with him. Before long the phone rang and it was his wife, wanting to know if he was there. He'd gone on an errand and when he didn't come back, she said, the logical place to call was the gallery. We laughed — it reminded us of the wife calling all the local bars, trying to track down her errant husband, only in this guy's case, she knew he would be here."

If indeed collecting is addictive, it is a happy malady from which dealers themselves are far from immune. Donna Hudgel commiserates, "In the book business, a common lament I hear among fellow dealers is, 'We could all have more money if we could just stop buying books.' But we can't stop buying books any more than our customers can stop buying books." "The problem," says Schwartz, is that "people come in every day offering you good deals and you've got to know to stop yourself from buying all the good deals. There's always twice as many things to buy as you'll have money for and the more knowledge you develop about it, the more of a danger you are to yourself. You say 'Oh! This was printed by so and so, it's really rare, worth a lot of money!' To everybody else it's just a $2 book, but because you know it's a special book, you buy it for $5 and store it against the time that a certain knowledgeable customer will also recognize that it's special and worth $10. The only thing is, the person who's going to buy that book from you may be living in New York City and may not get to your store until 2050. The profit is always insufficient — the prospecting is both the impediment to getting rich and the fun of it."

This incessant collecting, of course, is elective. If a person wants to turn a profit the opportunities are there, just as in any other business. But the profit motive is often secondary for collectors, who are primarily interested in finding and acquiring and adding to their personal collections. The means and ends become blurred and eventually indistinguishable. Besides, every upgrading acquisiton simply adds to the value of the business and in turn, builds equity for the dealer.

MAINTAINING THE LOVE AFFAIR

"It's hard when you're that close to something to always be having this love affair with it," says Joan Robey. "People have said, 'Do you really see all these beautiful things that are around you in the gallery all the time?' Well, lots of times I don't. Lots of times I walk in and look

around and instead of saying 'Wow — all this stuff is beautiful!' I say, 'Now
how are we going to make sales today?' It becomes your challenge rather
than your love. The time I do notice how beautiful things are is when I
have someone in the gallery, a customer who's looking and wants to
know something about this piece or that piece and then I get to converse
about it." Joan says that in conversing about a piece of art "I get in touch
with how beautiful it is," as if standing back and seeing the work afresh
through another's eyes allows her to feel the infatuation again. The ability to
share seems to be essential in keeping the whole venture from becoming
stagnant. New people, with their own viewpoints and experiences, infuse
collecting with the life the objects themselves might lose after a while.
Seeing that another person is moved by the same thing that touches you is
undeniably fulfilling. "It seems that what art does for someone is, it connects
them with something greater than themselves," reflects Kathe MacLaren.
"Very few other possessions can do that. It's like a really good book: It
touches a chord in you. We've seen people cry over an artist's work here in
the gallery."

GIVING OUR CHILDREN GOOD HOMES

When a collector has acquired something really special, maybe searched
a long time for it and delighted in just having it, it would be easy to
understand if he couldn't bear to part with it. On the other hand, these dealers
say that there is something uniquely gratifying about seeing a treasure go
to someone who obviously appreciates its value. "We get very proprie-
tary about books and if somebody wants a really neat book just to let
their kids cut pictures out of it, I'd probably not let them buy it,"
says Hudgel. "But if somebody's been searching for that book for ten
years and it's a cornerstone in their collection, then hey, that's absolutely
where it should go. Some books almost have somebody's name on them."
Pauli Wanderer smiles, "We always talk about 'giving our children good
homes.' Some dealers find it very difficult to sell, almost as if they're
owned by their collections. I've often felt, when I've sold something really
special, 'Oh, I wish I'd kept that,' but I'm always pleased when somebody
takes it home."

There's no way to get around the bittersweet ambivalence. For a true
collector, there will always be the desire to both keep and share the wonderful
finds. Still, the very decision to go into business tips the scales and the great
thing is these people have given themselves the option. Joan Markowitz feels
very strongly that fostering appreciation in others is the most satisfying part

of owning the gallery. "We have often said that there are certain pieces that are waiting for people and when we get them together it's wonderful."

Being in business provides great opportunities to do all the things collectors love: traveling, searching and finding, learning, meeting other enthusiasts, always finding new additions. Making money at it can be the icing, the *coup de grace*. Or as Joan Robey puts it, "a dream one can decide to make come true."

Retirement

"My idea of a great retirement is to do some traveling, go wherever I want to go, then come back home and work 24 hours a day. I love to work."

Thelton Skipper

If job satisfaction is one of the key elements of a long and happy life, one of the prime culprits in premature decline must be forced retirement. Men and women turned out of the work force while still in what they consider to be the prime of their lives often experience feelings of displacement, loss of identity and fears of dependency, all of which contribute to a decrease in emotional and physical well-being. Recognizing this, and the fact that age is not an obstacle when you work for yourself, increasing numbers of retirees are refusing to be put out to pasture; instead they are creating second careers for themselves in their own businesses. Moreover, many are finding that their own ventures are more interesting and fulfilling than the jobs they left.

AL SUTHERLAND, HOME SITTERS, INC.

Fifteen years ago Al Sutherland was a 66 year old, newly retired insurance man, chafing at the prospect of spending the rest of his life, "sitting on a shelf, waiting for the old man with the scythe." He was still healthy, alert, capable — and he wanted to do something with his energy and experience. What's more, he knew other retired men and women shared his feelings. He understood the two major problems confronting the retired: inflation and boredom. "There are a lot of things retired people can't do because of income. Unless people keep actively involved in life and living, they deteriorate both mentally and physically."

Al perceived a mutual need, as well as a mutual opportunity. He would establish a home sitting service — a service which would provide people to look after property, pets and plants while homeowners were away — and which would employ only retired people. The plan proved to be a boon to both his employees and his customers. The sitters love it, he says. "It brings them back to being useful human beings again. They feel needed and appreciated." And the customers? "They're delighted. All they need to do is pack their bags, call us and go."

Sutherland found a profitable solution to his retirement problem; others, following his lead, aren't waiting for the bestowal of senior citizenship to start planning something to occupy their later years. Today we see people in their forties and fifties already making plans to avoid the forced retirement trap.

FROM CHEMICAL ENGINEER TO WINEMAKER

Kenneth Moyer, president of the Moyer Texas Champagne Company, was 52 when he left his job as a chemical engineer to establish his own winery. Located in New Braunfels, Texas, a quiet town 30 miles north of San Antonio, Moyer's company enjoys the distinction of producing the state's first and only champagne.

While by no means a large operation — the plant is run for the most part by Moyer and a single helper — the company has flourished. Owing partly to the population's legendary love for an allegiance to all things Texan, Moyer says, establishing a local market for his wine has not been difficult. Moyer supplies some 48,000 bottles of wine annually to restaurants and hotels in major cities across the state.

State pride, however, has been only partly responsible for the enthusiastic reception of Moyer's wine. The biggest reason for its acceptance, he feels, has been the high quality of the product. "We use the Methode Champenoise, which is the most expensive and time-consuming method of making champagne. It requires several manufacturing steps that continue throughout the year; it generally takes 18 months to two years to produce a bottle ready for the table." For example, he points out, there is the process of disgorging, in which the yeast is removed from the neck of each bottle by hand. Imagine repeating this step 48,000 times and it becomes clear that the method isn't geared for high volume or quick profits. But then profit, counters Moyer, is not his chief goal anyway. "I'm not here to make a lot of money. I do it because I enjoy the work and I want to make a good wine."

From Industry to the Vineyard

Establishing the winery has been in a real sense a homecoming for Moyer and his wife, both of whom were born and raised in Texas. "I graduated from the University of Texas at Austin in the forties. I was married in

Kenneth Moyer, Texas Moyer Champagne Company

Austin; we had our first child in Austin." It was during his student years that Moyer first learned to make wine. "Back then, about the only thing we could afford to drink was the wine I made."

Moyer and his wife started the business in 1972, having made the decision to settle and put down roots after years of world travel. "I'm a chemical engineer by schooling. I worked with a German-American company and had been out of the country for some time. In '72, I had just finished a contract in Mexico City. My next contract was in Morocco." Because of family considerations, Moyer explains, he decided not to go. "We had had a child late in our lives; at that time she was about four years old and had never really lived in the States. I'd had vineyards before and we'd made wine for so long, we decided to plant vineyards and start a winery."

The family settled in Ohio, where they launched both a winery and a restaurant. In 1979 they decided to expand the business and bought property in New Braunfels with the idea of later selling their Ohio holdings and retiring in Texas.

"Retirement" is probably a misnomer, however. Moyer loves the detailed hands-on work of the winery — he calls himself "my own executive janitor" — and frankly states he has no intention of giving it up. "I never want to retire," he says. "I enjoy making the wine, meeting people every day. It's an enjoyable business. Besides, I don't know what the hell I'd do if I retired, anyway."

It's the Satisfaction that Counts

"Making a wine or a champagne is as much an art as it is a science; I don't claim to be an artist or a scientist, but there's something . . . ah, pleasing about doing this. Some people might say it isn't much, but the size of the place isn't what matters to me. I planted the vines, I grew the grapes, picked the grapes. I make the wine, sell the wine, I drink the wine myself. Making a product that people will love — that's satisfying.

"It's like the engineer who builds a bridge that people are going to cross for the next thousand years; I'm sure there's a lot of pleasure in that. It's the same thing with building a bottle of wine; I think we give a lot of people a lot of pleasure."

OF WOMEN AND RETIREMENT

Obviously, women need work satisfaction, whether in or outside the home, much the same as men. For most employed women, however, retirement is an issue more of livelihood than lifestyle. In fact, if she is single, a female retiree may have even more to lose than her male counterpart.

In the past it was the "empty-nest syndrome," retirement from childrearing, that most women had to reckon with. Today, for the growing numbers of divorced and never-married women facing retirement, the problem is fundamentally one of survival. Advances in equal opportunity notwithstanding, salaries even for professional women are roughly 60 percent those paid to men in the same jobs. Lower salaries mean fewer retirement benefits, smaller life insurance policies, fewer investments, smaller IRAs. Faced with inadequate Social Security allowances, single women over 65 may have no choice but to continue working somewhere. For many, self-employment offers a chance for livelihood and lifestyle that are equally comfortable.

"I'm not afraid of having to retire," declares Pauli Wanderer, a divorced mother of two teenagers. After she and her husband separated five years ago, Pauli and another woman opened an antique store. "You never retire out of this business," she says. "There are old timers in their seventies and eighties who are still going strong — I can stay in it till I drop dead! In the antique business there's always something to do, always something to learn. I could study a lifetime on any field in my business and not finish it. Glass, pottery, folk art, furniture, paintings, old books — I mean it's wonderful! I could just learn forever and it's all about things I love!"

FREEDOM TO PURSUE OTHER INTERESTS

Ralph Jackson cites the desire to perform volunteer service in his church as one of his major reasons for leaving a very lucrative salaried position. For Jackson, 42, the very problem was that retirement was still some time off; meanwhile, he and his family had things they wanted to do together.

In fact, Jackson still receives job offers from transit companies in major cities across the country. No doubt, another high-prestige, high-paying position could be his just for the formality of an interview. But that would miss the mark. He'd still be tied to a job in which income stopped when the time clock did; there would be no equity, no security apart from a place to "nine-to-five" it every day.

THELTON SKIPPER, A CHEERFUL WORKAHOLIC

"My idea of a great retirement," says Thelton Skipper, "is to travel — go wherever I want to go — then come back home and work 24 hours a day. I love to work." Skip, as he prefers to be called, is president and director of financial and investment planning of the Turnmar Financial Group. The basic goal of the firm, says Skipper, is to increase the net worth of the client by first reducing his tax liability and then investing the savings. "We call it 'affluency through education.' We help our clients understand what's available in the financial world, what avenues they can take, then we direct them into those areas."

One of the ways the program works is by taking the mystery out of tax shelters, financial-legal mechanisms that are, as Skip explains, actually quite straightforward and easy to understand. "You can never get rid of taxes, but you *can* postpone them with tax shelters or tax advantaged programs until other times in your life when you may be in a lower tax bracket. Say you're in a 50 percent tax bracket now and you're going to pay out a large chunk of your income in taxes. We try to find a legitimate way of reducing those taxes, then take the money that you were going to pay the government and put it in bonds, annuities, real estate — things that are relatively secure that will build money for you. At some future date when your tax liablity is lower, that money will still be there, only it's been making money for you all that time. The funds must be in a secure investment so that they're there when the time eventually comes that you must pay the taxes, but meanwhile, we're making interest on Uncle Sam's money.

"A Promotion into Poverty"

"It's taken me a long time to get here and I've done a lot of things on the way," says Skip, an affable North Carolinian who considers himself first and foremost a salesman. "It's always been a part of my blood that I loved to sell, to talk to people. I started at age nine, selling Christmas cards; I remember I made $100 that first year and I was thrilled. I've sold insurance, I've sold real estate, I've even been an auctioneer. I was an accountant for a short time, but I felt closed in — too much number-crunching and not enough people, not enough activity.

The impetus for launching his own financial planning business came when Skip received what he labels "a promotion into poverty." "I had made good money selling insurance on commission," he remembers. "As a salesman, I could make more money than the president of the company. Butthen I was transferred into the home office to train other salesmen; I was put on a salary and I starved to death." Conceivably, Skip could have chosen to return to the field, but the fact is, the financial issue was only part of his discontentment with working for the company.

"The hardest thing was adhering to policies into which I had no input. When you're in a company environment and somebody's paying you, you just have to do what they say even though you might disagree. That's especially hard when you're in a teaching position — I can't train somebody to go out and sell something I feel is wrong."

Thelton Skipper
Financial Consultant

"Plus, I like to be in charge. The problem with working in a company is you're not in charge. You feel like you're walled in when you can't make decisions. See, a good salesperson is creative. You take a creative person and put him on a strict salary with a strict set of rules and it destroys creativity." The solution, Skip decided, was to strike out on his own, to "go into a business where you can teach and train and do what you want to do."

Since Skipper launched his business on very little besides his ideas and his selling ability, the company's success is probably as good a testament as any to his understanding of how to make it in the financial world. "I started in this business with $2,000," he says. "My partner and I had a one-room office and we just hustled. We had to make it. Now our annual budget is over $200,000."

At first, the two men taught lots of public seminars. Dubbed "Success in the Eighties," the seminars dealt with basic financial principles. "I simply told people how I operate as a financial planner and investment adviser. Ninety percent of our clients in the beginning came from those seminars. Now those clients give us clients."

Although Skip happily confesses he "made more money last year than I ever dreamed possible," he is quick to point out the other payoffs that seem, to him, equally important.

"Independence is the biggest factor for me. I designed this business; I do things the way I want to, how and when I want to. I can control what we do, who we sell to, what products we use, how to plan, what types of financial planning we use. And it's my goals I'm working at. I have a partner but we think very much alike and we both happen to have the same goals.

"Clients demand time and you've got to be there when they want to see you, but you can always take time off if you need to. I like to take my vacations in slow times. I never take vacations at Christmas time or around income tax time. But again, we make that choice.

"Right now, there's a lot of travel involved, but it's because I choose to travel. I have control over that. If I don't want to take a client in California, I don't take it. We work with some professional athletes and those accounts take us out of town, but we don't have to go, we choose to."

The same reasoning, continues Skip, applies to the weekly time demands. "The person who wants to work nine to five shouldn't be in business for himself. He ought to work for somebody else on a salary because you can't do it working nine to five. Now if I want to be off, I take off — I took off yesterday afternoon for a birthday party for my little girl — but I'm here at seven in the morning and at ten, eleven o'clock at night and seven days a week. I worked Christmas, New Year's Eve and New Year's Day. That's what it takes if you want to make it."

But Skip is smiling broadly as he says all this, "Yeah! I made money!" he laughs.

It's the money, then, that makes it worthwhile? "Money helps but it's the accomplishment — knowing that you can do it and that you have done it. The most important thing is that you meet the challenges. If I didn't have a challenge I wouldn't do it."

Does he seriously never want to retire? He is kidding about that, right?

Skipper's smile fades and his round face takes on a determined expression. "I'm just as serious as I can be. I'll say it like Winston Churchill: 'Never, never.' I want to die sitting over there at my desk working with somebody. I told my wife that last night; that's where I'll die happy."

Recommended Reading

Note: A mail-order source for books, tapes and other materials on self-employment and career alternatives is The New Careers Center, P.O. Box 297, Boulder, CO 80306. Send your name and address for the current catalog/newsletter.

SPECIFIC SELF-EMPLOYMENT OPPORTUNITIES

Artist's Market, Diana Martin-Hoffman, ed. Writer's Digest Books, 9933
   Alliance Rd., Cincinnati, OH 45242 ($16.95).
*Bed & Breakfast: The Complete Guide to Starting a B&B in Your Home No
   Matter Where You Live,* Beverly Mathews. The New Careers Center,
   Box 297, Boulder, CO 80306 ($7.95).
*For Fun and Profit: Self-Employment Opportunities in Recreation, Sports
   and Travel,* Crawford Lindsey. Live Oak Publications, 6003 N. 51st St.,
   Boulder, CO 80301 ($9.95).
*Freelance Foodcrafting: How to Become Profitably Self-Employed in Your
   Own Creative Cooking Business,* Janet Shown. Live Oak Publications,
   6003 N. 51st St., Boulder, CO 80301 ($9.95).

From Rags to Riches: Success in Apparel Retailing, Marvin E. Segal. John Wiley & Sons, 605 Third Ave., New York, NY 10158 ($7.95).

How to Be a Freelance Photographer, Ted Schwarz. Contemporary Books, Inc., 180 North Michigan Ave., Chicago, IL 60601 ($4.95).

How to Make Money in the Antiques-Collectibles Business. Houghton-Mifflin, Two Park St., Boston, MA 02108 ($10.95).

How to Make Money With Your Micro. John Wiley & Sons, 605 Third Ave., New York, NY 10158 ($14.95).

How to Make Money With Your Video Camera, T. Schwartz. Prentice-Hall, Englewood Cliffs, NJ 07632 ($9.95).

How to Open and Run a Money-Making Travel Aency. John Wiley & Sons, 605 Third Ave., New York, NY 10158 ($8.95).

How to Open and Successfully Operate a Country Inn, Karen Etsell with Elaine Brennan. Berkshire Traveller Press, Stockbridge, MA 01262 ($8.95).

How to Run a Successful Florist and Plant Store, Bram Cavin. John Wiley & Sons, 605 Third Ave., New York, NY 10158 ($14.95).

How to Start a Professional Photography Business, Ted Schwarz. Contemporary Books, Inc., 180 North Michigan Ave., Chicago, IL 60601 ($9.95).

How to Start and Operate a Mail-Order Business, Julian L. Simon. McGraw-Hill, 1221 Ave. of the Americas, New York, NY 10020 ($19.95).

How to Start and Run Your Own Word Processing Business. John Wiley & Sons, 605 Third Ave., New York, NY 10158 ($8.95).

How We Made a Million Dollars Recycling Great Old Houses, Sam and Mary Weir. Contemporary Books, Inc., 180 North Michigan Ave., Chicago, IL 60601 ($8.95).

Ideas That Work: 10 of Today's Most Exciting and Profitable Self-Employment Opportunities, Susan Elliott. Live Oak Publications, 6003 N. 51st Street, Boulder, CO 80301 ($9.95).

Kids Mean Business: How to Turn Your Love of Children Into a Profitable and Wonderfully Satisfying Business, Barbralu Manning. Live Oak Publications, 6003 N. 51st St., Boulder, CO 80301 ($9.95).

Making Money Making Music, James Dearing. Writer's Digest Books, 9933 Alliance Rd., Cincinnati, OH 45242 ($12.95).

Opening Your Own Retail Store, Lyn Taetzsch. Contemporary Books, Inc., 180 North Michigan Ave., Chicago, IL 60601 ($9.95).

Pouring for Profit: A Guide to Bar and Beverage Management, Costas Katsigris and Mary Porter. John Wiley & Sons, 605 Third Ave., New York, NY 10158 ($16.95).

Raising Animals For Fun and Profit, the Editors of "Countryside Magazine." TAB Books, Blue Ridge Summit, PA 17214 ($13.95).

Sell and Re-Sell Your Photos, Rohn Engh. Writer's Digest Books, 9933 Alliance Rd., Cincinnati, OH 45242 ($14.95).

Start and Run a Profitable Craft Business, William G. Hyne. TAB Books, Blue Ridge Summit, PA 17214 ($10.95).

Start and Run a Profitable Video Store: A Complete Step-By-Step Business Plan, Stan Loh. TAB Books, Blue Ridge Summit, PA 17214 ($10.95).

Step Into Sales: 6 Weeks to Successful Direct Selling From Your Home, Claire M. Cleaver. Avon Books, 1790 Broadway, New York, NY 10019 ($8.95).

The #1 Home Business Book, George and Sandra Delany. Liberty Publishing Company, 50 Scott Adam Rd., Cockeysville, MD 21030 ($4.95).

The Business of Being a Writer, Stephen Goldin and Kathleen Sky. The New Careers Center, Box 297, Boulder, CO 80306 ($13.95).

How to Open and Run a Money-Making Travel Agency. John Wiley & Sons, 605 Third Ave., New York, NY 10158 ($8.95).

GENERAL BUSINESS INFORMATION

Buying Your Own Small Business, Brian R. Smith and Thomas L. West. Viking/Penguin, Inc., 40 West 23rd Street, New York, NY 10010-5201 ($21.95).

Raising Seed Money for Your Own Business, Brian R. Smith. Viking/Penguin, Inc., 40 West 23rd Street, New York, NY 10010-5201 ($19.95).

The New Financial Guide for the Self-Employed, John Ellis. Contemporary Books, Inc., 180 North Michigan Ave., Chicago, IL 60601 ($7.95).

The Source Book of Franchise Opportunities, Robert E. Bond. Dow Jones-Irwin, Homewood, IL 60430 ($19.95).

Index